ROAST
IT

ROAST IT

IT

There's Nothing Better Than a Delicious Roast

STERLING EPICURE
New York

STERLING EPICURE
New York

An Imprint of Sterling Publishing
1166 Avenue of the Americas
New York, NY 10036

STERLING EPICURE is a trademark of Sterling
Publishing Co., Inc. The distinctive Sterling logo
is a registered trademark of Sterling Publishing
Co., Inc.

First published in the United Kingdom in 2013 by
Pavilion Books Company Limited

First Sterling edition published in 2015

© 2013 by The National Magazine Company
Limited and Collins & Brown

ISBN 978-1-4549-1772-4

Distributed in Canada by Sterling Publishing
c/o Canadian Manda Group, 664 Annette Street
Toronto, Ontario, Canada M6S 2C8

For information about custom editions, special
sales, and premium and corporate purchases,
please contact Sterling Special Sales at 800-805-
5489 or specialsales@sterlingpublishing.com.

Manufactured in China

2 4 6 8 10 9 7 5 3 1

www.sterlingpublishing.com

NOTES: Ovens and broilers must be preheated to
the specified temperature.

Large eggs should be used except where otherwise
specified. Free-range eggs are recommended.

Note that some recipes contain raw or lightly
cooked eggs. The young, elderly, pregnant women,
and anyone with an immune-deficiency disease
should avoid these because of the slight risk of
salmonella.

Contents

Perfect Poultry

Perfect Preparation

Chicken and other poultry, such as turkey and duck, are perfect for roasting. Roasting is also a simple way to cook young game birds.

Preparing the bird

Take the bird out of the refrigerator 45 minutes–1 hour before roasting to let it reach room temperature. Before stuffing a bird for roasting, clean it thoroughly. Put the bird in the sink and pull out and discard any loose fat with your fingers. Then dry the bird well using paper towels.

Trussing

It is not essential to truss poultry before roasting it, but it gives the bird a neater shape for serving at the table.

1 Cut out the wishbone by pulling back the flap of skin at the neck end and locating the tip of the bone with a small sharp knife. Run the knife along the inside of the bone on both sides, then on the outside. Take care not to cut deep into the breast meat. Using poultry shears or sharp-pointed scissors, snip the tip of the bone from the breastbone and pull the bone away from the breast. Snip the two ends or pull them out by hand.

1

2 Pull off any loose fat from the neck or cavity. Put the wing tips under the breast and fold the neck flap onto the back of the bird. Thread a trussing needle and use it to secure the neck flap.

3 Push a metal skewer through both legs, at the joint between thigh and drumstick. Twist some string around both ends of the skewer and pull firmly to tighten.

4 Turn the bird over. Bring the string over the ends of the drumsticks, pull tight, and tie to secure the legs.

Hygiene

- ❏ Raw poultry and meat contain harmful bacteria that can spread easily to anything they touch.
- ❏ Always wash your hands, kitchen surfaces, cutting boards, knives, and other equipment before and after handling poultry or meat.
- ❏ Don't let raw poultry or meat touch other raw or cooked foods.
- ❏ Always cover raw poultry and meat and store in the bottom of the refrigerator, where they can't touch or drip on to other foods.

2

3

Poultry and Game Perfect Roasting

Basting

Chicken, turkey, and other poultry need to be basted regularly during roasting to keep the flesh moist. Use an oven mitt to steady the roasting pan, then spoon the juices and melted fat over the top of the bird. Alternatively, use a bulb baster.

How to tell if poultry is cooked through

☐ To check if chicken or turkey is cooked, pierce the thickest part of the meat—usually the thigh—with a skewer. The juices that run out should be golden and clear. If there are any traces of pink in the juice, put the bird back into the oven and roast 10 minutes longer, then check again.

☐ Duck and game birds are traditionally served with the meat slightly pink: if overcooked, the meat can be dry.

Resting

Once the bird is cooked, leave it to rest before carving. Lift it out of the roasting pan, put it on a plate and cover loosely with foil and a clean dish towel. Resting lets the juices to settle back into the meat, leaving it moist and easier to carve.

Resting times

Grouse and small game birds	10 minutes
Chicken and duck	15 minutes
Turkey and goose	up to 1¼ hours

Poultry and game roasting times

Chicken

To calculate the roasting time for a chicken, weigh the oven-ready bird after stuffing, (if using) and allow 20 minutes per 1lb. (450g), plus 20 minutes extra, in an oven heated to 400°F (350°F convection oven).

OVEN-READY WEIGHT	SERVES	COOKING TIME (APPROX.)
3–3½lb. (1.4–1.6 kg)	4–6	1½ hours
4–5lb. (1.8–2.3kg)	6–8	1 hour 50 minutes
5½–6lb. (2.5–2.7kg)	8–10	2¼ hours

Turkey

Wrap loosely in a "tent" of foil, then roast in an oven heated to 375°F (325°F convection oven). Allow 20 minutes per 1lb. (450g), plus 20 minutes extra. Remove the foil about 1 hour before the end of the roasting time to brown. Baste regularly.

OVEN-READY WEIGHT	SERVES	COOKING TIME (APPROX.)	
5–8lb. (2.3–3.6kg)	4–8	15–18 hours	2–3 hours
8–11lb. (3.6–5kg)	8–11	18–20 hours	3–3¼ hours
11–15lb. (5–6.8kg)	11–15	20–24 hours	3¼–4 hours
15–20lb. (6.8–9kg)	15–20	24–30 hours	4–5½ hours

Other poultry

Heat the oven to 400°F (350°F convection oven).

	SERVES	COOKING TIME (APPROX.)	
Squab	1–2	20 minutes per 1lb. (450g)	
Guinea fowl	3lb. (1.4kg)	3–4	1½ hours
Duck	4–5½lb. (1.8–2.5kg)	2–4	1½–2 hours
Goose, small	8–12lb. (3.6–5.4kg)	4–7	20 minutes per 1lb. (450g)
Goose, medium	12–14lb. (5.4–6.3kg)	8–11	25 minutes per 1lb. (450g)

Feathered game

Heat the oven to 400°F (350°F convection oven).

	SERVES	COOKING TIME (APPROX.)
Grouse	1–2	25–35 minutes
Partridge	2	20–25 minutes
Pheasant	2–4	45–60 minutes

Perfect Carving

Follow these tried-and-true steps for perfect carving results.

After resting, put the bird on a carving board.

1   Steady the bird with a carving fork. To cut breast meat, start at the neck end and cut slices about ¼in. (0.5cm) thick. Use the carving knife and fork to lift them onto a warm serving plate.

2   To cut off the legs, cut the skin between the thigh and breast.

3   Pull the leg down to expose the joint between the thigh bone and rib cage and cut through that joint.

4   Cut through the joint between the thigh and drumstick.

5   To carve meat from the leg (for turkeys and very large chickens), remove it from the carcass and joint the two parts of the leg (step 4). Holding the drumstick by the thin end, stand it up on the carving board and carve slices roughly parallel with the bone. The thigh can be carved either flat on the board or upright.

Squab and small game birds

Squab and other small birds, such as grouse, serve one or two people. To serve two, you will need to split them. The easiest way to do this is with poultry shears and using a carving fork to steady the bird. Insert the shears between the legs and cut through the breastbone. As you do this, the bird will open out, exposing the backbone; cut through the backbone.

Storing leftovers

Don't forget the leftovers when the meal is finished—never leave poultry standing in a warm room. Cool quickly in a cold place, then cover and chill.

Roast Chicken with Stuffing and Gravy

Prep time: 30 minutes
Cooking time: about 1 hour 20 minutes, plus cooling and resting

3lb. (1.4kg) chicken

2 garlic cloves

1 onion, cut into wedges

2 tsp. kosher salt

2 tsp. freshly ground black pepper

4 fresh parsley sprigs

4 fresh tarragon sprigs

2 bay leaves

4 tbsp. butter, cut into cubes

For the stuffing

3 tbsp. butter

1 small onion, chopped

1 garlic clove, crushed

1½ cups fresh white bread crumbs

finely grated zest and juice
of 1 small lemon, halves put to one
side for the chicken

2 tbsp. each freshly chopped flat-leaf
parsley and tarragon

1 large egg yolk

salt and freshly ground black pepper

For the gravy

¾ cup + 2 tbsp. (200ml) dry white wine

1 tbsp. Dijon mustard

2 cups (450ml) hot chicken stock
(see page 155)

2 tbsp. butter, mixed with 2 tbsp.
all-purpose flour

1   Heat the oven to 375°F (325°F
convection oven). To make the
stuffing, melt the butter in a pan and
fry the onion and garlic for 5—10
minutes until soft. Cool, then stir in
the remaining ingredients, adding
the egg yolk last. Season well with salt
and pepper.

2   Put the chicken on a board breast-side
up, then put the garlic, onion, reserved
lemon halves, half the kosher salt, the
pepper, and half the herb sprigs into
the cavity.

3   Lift the loose skin at the neck and fill

14

the cavity with the stuffing. Turn the bird over onto its breast and pull the neck flap down and over the opening to cover the stuffing. Rest the wing tips across it and truss the chicken (see page 8). Weigh the stuffed bird to calculate the cooking time (see page 11).

4 Put the chicken on a rack in a roasting pan. Season, then add the remaining herbs and the bay leaves. Dot with the butter and roast, basting halfway through, until cooked through and the juices run clear when the thickest part of the thigh is pierced with a skewer. If there are any traces of pink in the juice, put the bird back into the oven and roast for 10 minutes longer, then check again in the same way.

5 Transfer the chicken to a serving dish, cover loosely with foil, and leave to rest while you make the gravy. Tilt the roasting pan and pour off all but about 3 tbsp. fat. Put the pan on the stovetop over high heat, add the wine, and boil for 2 minutes. Add the mustard and hot stock, and bring back to a boil. Gradually whisk in knobs of the butter mixture until smooth, then season with salt and ground black pepper. Carve the chicken and serve with the stuffing and gravy.

Serves 4

Summer Roast Chicken

Prep time: 25 minutes
Cooking time: about 1¾ hours, plus resting

3½oz. (100g) feta, crumbled

⅓ cup pitted and sliced black olives

2 fresh oregano sprigs, leaves stripped
and finely chopped

1 tbsp. olive oil

3½lb. (1.6kg) chicken

1 lemon, halved

11oz. (300g) cherry tomatoes

scant ¾ cup couscous

a large handful of watercress

salt and freshly ground black pepper

1   Heat the oven to 375°F (325°F
convection oven). Put half the feta,
half the olives, half the oregano, and
the oil into a small bowl with plenty
of ground black pepper and stir
together. Set aside.

2   Lift up the neck flap of the chicken
and use your fingers to ease the skin
gently away from the breast meat—
work all the way down the sides of the
breasts and toward the legs. Push the
feta mixture between the skin and
meat to cover the whole breast area.

Pull the neck flap down and over
and secure with a skewer or cocktail
picks. Put a lemon half in the cavity
of the chicken.

3   Put the chicken into a medium-
large roasting pan and drizzle the
remaining oil over. Season and roast
for 1¼ hours. Add the tomatoes to the
pan and shake to coat them in the oil,
then return to the oven for 15 minutes
longer, or until the chicken is cooked
through and the tomatoes burst.

4   Carefully transfer the chicken
to a board and put the tomatoes into
a small serving bowl. Cover both with
foil. Tilt the roasting pan and spoon
off as much fat as possible, leaving
behind the darker juices. Add the
couscous to the roasting pan and stir
to coat. Squeeze in the juice from the
remaining lemon half, then pour
in just enough boiling water to cover
the couscous. Cover the pan tightly
with plastic wrap and leave to stand
for 10 minutes.

5 Fluff up the couscous with a fork and stir the watercress and remaining feta, olives, and oregano. Check the seasoning.

6 Leave the chicken to rest for at least 25 minutes before serving with the couscous and tomatoes.

SAVE EFFORT

Save on dish washing by making the couscous in the pan you've used to roast the chicken—it adds great flavor, too.

Serves 4

Roast Curried Chicken

Prep time: 20 minutes
Cooking time: about 1½ hours, plus resting

2in. (5cm) piece fresh ginger root

4lb. (1.8kg) chicken

1 lime, halved

3 tbsp. butter, softened

2 tbsp. mild curry paste

1¾lb. (800g) new potatoes

¾ tbsp. all-purpose flour

⅔ cup (160ml) coconut milk

1 tsp. brown sugar (optional)

salt and freshly ground black pepper

seasonal vegetables to serve

1   Heat the oven to 375°F (325°F convection oven). Roughly chop half the ginger root (leave the skin on) and put into the cavity of the bird. Add the lime halves and tie the legs together. Put the chicken into a large roasting pan. Put the butter and half the curry paste into a small bowl and mix together. Spread over the top and sides of the bird. Cover with foil and roast for 40 minutes.

2   Carefully remove the foil and add the potatoes to the pan, turning them to coat in the buttery mixture. Put the pan back into the oven and roast the chicken for 40 minutes longer, or until the potatoes are tender and the chicken is cooked through. Lift the chicken out of the pan and put on a board. Cover loosely with foil and leave to rest. Put the potatoes into a serving dish and keep warm.

3   Tilt the roasting pan and spoon off and discard most of the fat. Put the pan on the stovetop over medium heat and stir in the flour and remaining curry paste, then grate in the remaining ginger root. Stirring constantly, add the coconut milk. Fill the empty coconut can with water and add it to the pan. Bring to a boil, then reduce the heat to low and simmer, stirring, for 3–5 minutes until the mixture thickens. Check the seasoning and add the sugar, if needed. Serve the chicken, roasted potatoes, and gravy with seasonal vegetables.

Serves 4

Clementine and Sage Turkey with Madeira Gravy

Prep time: 30 minutes
Cooking time: about 3 hours 40 minutes, plus resting

12lb. (5.4kg) free-range turkey (set aside the giblets for stock, if you like—see page 156. Buy the best quality turkey you can to get the maximum flavor and texture)

3 firm clementines

¾oz. (20g) fresh sage

7 tbsp. butter, softened

enough stuffing for 8 portions (see pages 28–30)

3 celery stalks

3 carrots, halved lengthwise

salt and freshly ground black pepper

fried clementine halves and stuffing balls to garnish (optional)

For the Madeira Gravy

2 tbsp. all-purpose flour

½ cup (125ml) Madeira wine

1¼ cups (300ml) chicken stock (see page 155)

1 tbsp. honey or red currant jelly, if needed

1 Remove the turkey from the refrigerator 1 hour before you stuff it to let it come to room temperature.

2 Heat the oven to 375°F (325°F convection oven). Finely grate the zest from the clementines into a bowl. Halve the zest-free clementines and put to one side. Next, add 2 tbsp. thinly sliced sage leaves (put the rest of the bunch to one side) to the bowl with the butter and plenty of seasoning and mix well.

3 Put the turkey, breast-side up, on a board. Use tweezers to pluck any feathers from the skin. Loosen the skin at the neck end and use your fingers to ease the skin away from the breast meat, until 3½in. (9cm) is free. Spread most of the flavoured butter between the skin and meat. Put the remaining flavored butter to one side.

4 Spoon the cold stuffing into the neck cavity, pushing it down between the skin and breast meat and taking care not to overfill. Neaten the shape. Turn the turkey over onto its breast, pull the neck flap down and over the stuffing and secure the neck skin with a skewer or cocktail picks. Weigh the stuffed turkey and calculate the cooking time, allowing 30–35 minutes per 2¼lb. (1kg).

5 Make a platform in a large roasting pan with celery stalks and carrot halves and sit the turkey on top. Put the clementine halves and the remaining sage (stems and all) into the turkey cavity, then rub the remaining flavored butter over the breast of the bird. Tie the legs together with string, season the bird all over, and cover loosely with foil.

6 Roast for the calculated time, removing the foil for the last 45 minutes of cooking, and basting at least three times during roasting. If the skin is browning too quickly, cover with foil again.

7 To check if the turkey is cooked through, pierce the thickest part of the thigh with a skewer—the juices should run clear. If there are any traces of pink in the juice, put the bird back into the oven and roast for 10 minutes longer, then check again. Alternatively, use a meat thermometer—the temperature needs to read 172°F when inserted into the thickest part of the breast.

8 When the turkey is cooked, tip the bird so the juices run into the pan, then transfer the turkey to a board. (Put the roasting pan to one side to make the Maderia Gravy in.) Cover the turkey loosely with foil and clean dish towels to help keep the heat in. Leave to rest in a warm place for at least 30 minutes, or up to 1¼ hours.

9 To make the gravy, tilt the roasting pan and spoon off most of the fat, leaving the vegetables in the pan. Put the pan on the stovetop over medium heat and add the flour. Cook, stirring well with a wooden spoon, for 1 minute. Gradually add the Madeira, scraping up all the sticky bits from the bottom of the pan, then leave to bubble for a few minutes. Next, stir in the stock and leave to simmer, stirring occasionally, for 5 minutes. Check the seasoning and add the honey or red currant jelly, if needed. Strain into a warm gravy boat, or into a clean pan to reheat when needed.

10 To serve, unwrap the turkey and transfer to a warm serving plate. Remove the skewer or cocktail picks and garnish with the fried clementine halves and stuffing balls, if you like. Carve and serve with the gravy.

SAVE TIME

Prepare the turkey to the end of step 5 up to one day ahead. Chill. Leave the stuffed turkey to come to room temperature, then complete the recipe to serve.

Serves 8,
with leftovers

Lemon-and-Parsley Butter Roast Turkey

Prep time: 25 minutes
Cooking time: about 3½ hours, plus resting

12lb. (5.4kg) free-range turkey (put the giblets for stock to one side—see page 156. Buy the best quality turkey you can to get the maximum flavor and texture)

1 lemon, zested and halved

7 tbsp. unsalted butter, softened

¾oz. (20g) fresh flat-leaf parsley, finely chopped

1 quantity uncooked Herbed Bread Stuffing (see page 26)

1 red onion, halved

5 fresh bay leaves (optional)

salt and freshly ground black pepper

fresh bay leaves and 4 lemon halves, browned, cut-side down, in oil, to garnish

1 Remove the turkey from the refrigerator 1 hour before you stuff it to let it come to room temperature.

2 Heat the oven to 375°F (325°F convection oven). Put the lemon zest, butter, parsley, and plenty of seasoning into a small bowl and mix well.

3 Put the turkey, breast-side up, on a board. Use tweezers to pluck any feathers from the skin. Loosen the skin at the neck end and use your fingers to ease the skin gently away from breast meat, until about 3½in. (9cm) is free. Spread the butter mixture between the skin and meat.

4 Spoon the cold stuffing into the neck cavity, pushing it down between the skin and breast meat and taking care not to overfill. Neaten the shape. Turn the turkey over onto its breast, pull the neck flap down and over the stuffing, and secure the neck

skin with a skewer or cocktail picks. Weigh the turkey and calculate the cooking time, allowing 30–35 minutes per 2¼lb. (1kg).

5 Transfer the turkey to a large roasting pan. Cut the zested lemon in half and squeeze the juice over the bird. Put the juiced halves into the bird's cavity, together with the red onion halves and the bay leaves, if you like. Tie the legs together with string, season the bird all over, and cover loosely with foil.

6 Roast the turkey for the calculated time, removing the foil for the last 30 minutes of cooking, and basting at least four times during roasting. If the skin is browning too quickly, cover with foil again.

7 To check if the turkey is cooked through, pierce the thickest part of the thigh with a skewer—the juices should run clear. If there are any traces of pink in the juice, put the bird back into the oven and roast for 10 minutes longer, then check again in the same way. Alternatively, use a meat thermometer—the temperature needs to read 172°F when inserted into thickest part of the breast.

8 When the turkey is cooked, tip the bird so the juices run into the pan, then transfer the turkey to a board (put the roasting pan for the gravy to one side; see page 158). Cover well with foil and clean dish towels to help keep the heat in, then leave to rest in a warm place for at least 30 minutes, or up to 1¼ hours.

9 When ready to serve, put the bird on a warm plate or board, remove the string, skewer or cocktail picks and garnish, if you like, with browned lemons and bay leaves.

Serves 8, with leftovers

Herbed Bread Stuffing

Prep time: 20 minutes
Cooking time: about 45 minutes, plus cooling

6 tbsp. butter, plus extra to top the stuffing

1 onion, finely chopped

10 cups fresh white bread crumbs

1 tbsp. Italian herbs

2¼ cups (525ml) vegetable stock (see page 154)

8 tbsp. freshly chopped mixed herbs, such as parsley, cilantro, thyme, sage, and mint, plus extra to garnish

2 celery stalks, finely chopped

2 crisp dessert apples, such as Braeburn, skin on, cored, and finely diced

1 tbsp. ready-toasted and chopped hazelnuts

4 smoked bacon slices (optional)

salt and freshly ground black pepper

1 Heat the oven to 375°F (325°F convection oven) mark 5. Heat the butter in a large skillet and slowly fry the onion for 10 minutes, or until soft. Stir in the bread crumbs and mix to combine. Next add the Italian herbs and pour in the stock.

2 Mix in the fresh herbs, celery, apples, and hazelnuts, and check the seasoning (don't stir too much or the stuffing might be too gluey). Put enough of the stuffing to one side for the turkey.

3 Spoon the remaining stuffing into a baking dish suitable for serving from (add some extra stock if you prefer your stuffing looser) and top with the extra butter. Lay the bacon strips on top, if you like.

4 Cook the stuffing in the baking dish for 30 minutes, or until the bacon is crisp and the stuffing is piping hot. Serve garnished with the herb leaves.

Prepare to the end of step 2 up to 5 hours ahead. Put enough of the stuffing to one side for the turkey. With the remaining stuffing, either complete to end of step 3, then cover and chill, or form into balls, wrap in bacon strips, and put on a baking sheet. Complete the recipe to serve.

Serves 8

Perfect Stuffing

These stuffings are suitable for chicken, turkey, or goose.
All can be made a day ahead and chilled overnight. Alternatively—
with the exception of the wild rice stuffing—all can be frozen for up to one
month. Thaw overnight in the refrigerator before using to stuff the bird.

Orange, Sage, and Thyme Stuffing

To serve eight, you will need:
2 tbsp. olive oil; 1 large finely chopped onion; 2 crushed garlic cloves;
1½ cups fresh white bread crumbs; ½ cup toasted and chopped pine nuts; grated zest of 1 orange; 2–3 tbsp. orange juice; 1 beaten large egg yolk; 2 tbsp. freshly chopped thyme; 2 tbsp. freshly chopped sage; salt and freshly ground black pepper.

1 Heat the oil and fry the onion and garlic slowly for 5 minutes, or until soft but not brown.
2 Put the remaining ingredients into a large bowl. Add the onion mixture, season and stir to bind, adding more orange juice, if needed.

Rosemary and Lemon Stuffing

To serve four to six, you will need:
2 tbsp. butter; 1 finely chopped onion; 2 heaped cups fresh white bread crumbs; 1 tbsp. freshly chopped rosemary leaves; grated zest of 1 lemon; 1 beaten large egg; salt and freshly ground black pepper.

1 Melt the butter in a skillet, then fry the onion over low heat for about 10 minutes until soft and golden. Tip into a bowl and leave to cool.
2 Add the bread crumbs, rosemary leaves, and lemon zest to the onion. Season well, then add the egg and stir to bind.

Bacon, Pecan, and Wild Rice Stuffing

To serve eight, you will need:
3¾ cups (900ml) hot chicken stock (see page 155); 1 bay leaf; 1 fresh thyme sprig; heaped 1 cup mixed long-grain and wild rice; 4 tbsp. unsalted butter; 8oz. (225g) roughly chopped smoked bacon; 2 finely chopped onions; 3 finely chopped celery stalks; ½ Savoy cabbage, chopped; 3 tbsp. freshly chopped marjoram; heaped ½ cup packaged sage and onion stuffing mix; 1 cup chopped pecans; salt and freshly ground black pepper.

1   Pour the stock into a pan, add the bay leaf and thyme, and bring to a boil. Add the rice and cover the pan, then reduce the heat and cook according to the package directions. Drain, if necessary, then tip into a large bowl and cool quickly, discarding the herbs.
2   Melt the butter in a large pan, add the bacon, onions, and celery, and cook over medium heat for 10 minutes, or until the onions are soft but not brown. Add the cabbage and marjoram and cook for 5 minutes, stirring regularly.
3   Add the cabbage mixture to the rice, together with the stuffing mix and pecans. Tip into a bowl, season to taste and cool quickly.

Sausage, Cranberry, and Apple Stuffing

To serve eight, you will need:
4 tbsp. butter; 1 finely chopped onion; 1 crushed garlic clove; 10oz. (275g) pork link sausages (about 4), skinned and broken up; ½ cup dried cranberries; 2 tbsp. freshly chopped parsley; 1 red dessert apple; salt and freshly ground black pepper.

1   Heat the butter in a pan, add the onion, and fry over medium heat for 5 minutes, or until soft. Add the garlic and cook for 1 minute. Tip into a bowl and leave to cool. Add the sausages, cranberries, and parsley, then cover and chill overnight, or freeze.
2   Core and chop the apple, then add it to the stuffing. Season with salt and ground black pepper and stir well.

Pork, Chestnut, and Orange Stuffing

To serve eight to ten, you will need:
4 tbsp. butter; 6 roughly chopped shallots; 4 roughly chopped celery stalks; 1 snipped fresh rosemary sprig; 1 tbsp. freshly chopped flat-leaf parsley; 3 cups firm white bread cut into rough dice; 8oz. (225g) cooking apples (2 apples), peeled, cored, and chopped; ⅔ cup cooked and peeled (or vacuum-packed) chestnuts, roughly chopped; grated zest of 1 large orange; 1lb. (450g) coarse pork sausage meat; salt and freshly ground black pepper.

1   Melt the butter in a large skillet and fry the shallots, celery, and rosemary slowly for 10–12 minutes until the vegetables are soft and golden. Tip into a large bowl. Add the parsley, bread, apples, chestnuts ,and orange zest to the bowl. Season and mix well.
2   Divide the sausage meat into walnut-size pieces. Fry, in batches, until golden and cooked through. Add to the bowl and stir to mix, then cool quickly.

Pork, Spinach, and Apple Stuffing

To serve eight, you will need:
2 tbsp. olive oil; 1 cup finely chopped onion; 8oz. (225g) fresh spinach, torn into pieces if the leaves are large; 2 sharp apples, such as Granny Smith, peeled, cored, and cut into chunks; 14oz. (400g) pork sausage meat; coarsely grated zest of 1 lemon; 1 tbsp. freshly chopped thyme; 2 cups fresh white bread crumbs; 2 large eggs, beaten; salt and freshly ground black pepper.

1   Heat the oil in a skillet, add the onion, and fry for 10 minutes, or until soft. Increase the heat, add the spinach, and cook until it wilts.
2   Add the apples and cook, stirring, for 2–3 minutes, then leave to cool. When the mixture is cold, add the sausage meat, lemon zest, thyme, bread crumbs, and eggs, then season with salt and ground black and stir until evenly mixed.

Falafel Balls

These stuffing balls are delicious served with turkey, but are also great with pita bread and a salad to make a vegetarian meal.

To serve eight to ten, you will need: scant 1½ cups dried chickpeas; 1 small roughly chopped onion; a small handful of fresh cilantro; 3 roughly chopped garlic cloves; the juice of ½ lemon; 2 tsp. ground cumin; ½ tsp. baking soda; olive oil to shallow-fry; salt and freshly ground black pepper.

1 Put the chickpeas into a pan and cover with plenty of cold water. Bring to a boil and boil for 2 minutes, then leave to soak for 2 hours. Drain.

2 Put the drained chickpeas into a food processor with the onion, cilantro, garlic, lemon juice, cumin, baking soda, ½ tsp. salt and ground black pepper to taste. Blend until everything is finely ground and beginning to stick together. Take small handfuls of the mixture and squeeze in the palm of your hand to extract any excess moisture. Shape into walnut-size balls.

3 Heat the oil in a skillet over medium-high heat and fry the falafel for 3–4 minutes until they turn a deep golden brown all over. Drain well on paper towels. Serve immediately, or chill for later use.

4 To serve with a roast bird or meat, put the falafel in a kitchen foil package and reheat alongside the roast for 15–20 minutes.

Turkey Breast with Sausage, Cranberry, and Apple Stuffing

🍴 **Prep time:** 25 minutes
Cooking time: about 1½ hours, plus resting

3lb. (1.4kg) turkey breast roast

Sausage, Cranberry, and Apple Stuffing, thawed (see page 29)

3 tbsp. olive oil

1–2 tsp. poultry seasoning

1 red dessert apple

4–5 bay leaves

salt and freshly ground black pepper

For the gravy

1 tbsp. all-purpose flour

2 tbsp. cranberry jelly

1¼ cups (300ml) hard cider or apple juice

2½ cups (600ml) hot chicken stock (see page 155)

1 Heat the oven to 400°F (350°F convection oven). Put three or four wooden skewers into a bowl of water to soak.

2 Put the turkey joint on a board, skin-side down, and cut down the middle, along the length of the breast, to just over three-quarters of the way through. Season with salt and ground black pepper, spoon the stuffing inside, then push the breast back together. Secure with string and the soaked skewers. Weigh the stuffed breast, then calculate the cooking time, allowing 20 minutes per 1lb. (450g), plus 20 minutes extra. For the specified 3lb. (1.4kg) turkey, the cooking time will be about 1 hour 20 minutes.

3 Put the breast into a roasting pan, skin-side up, drizzle with the oil, and sprinkle with the poultry seasoning. Cover with foil and put into the oven.

4 Core the apple and cut into thin round slices. About 30 minutes before the end of the roasting time, remove the foil and push the apple slices and bay leaves under the string around

the breast. Roast, uncovered, for the final 30 minutes, or until cooked through—the juices should run clear when the thickest part of the meat is pierced with a skewer. If there are any traces of pink in the juice, put the breast back into the oven and roast for 10 minutes longer, then check again in the same way.

5   Transfer the turkey breast to a warm plate, cover with foil, and leave to rest for about 20 minutes.

6   To make the gravy, tilt the roasting pan and drain off all but about 1 tbsp. fat. Add the flour and stir in. Put the pan on the stovetop over medium heat and cook for 1 minute, scraping the pan to mix in all the juices. Stir in the cranberry jelly and cider, bring to a boil, and bubble until the liquid reduces by half. Add the stock and cook for about 5 minutes until the gravy thickens slightly. Remove the skewers from the turkey, cut the meat into slices, and serve with the gravy.

Serves 8

Squab with Pancetta, Artichokes, and Potato Salad

Prep time: 20 minutes, plus overnight marinating
Cooking time: 1 hour 40 minutes, plus resting

grated zest of 1 lemon

5 large fresh rosemary sprigs, leaves stripped

4 tbsp. white wine vinegar

⅔ cup (160ml) fruity white wine

4 garlic cloves, crushed

3 tbsp. freshly chopped oregano or 1 tsp dried oregano

11oz. (300g) marinated artichokes in olive oil, drained, oil put to one side

3 squab chickens (each weighing about 1lb./450g)

½ tsp. cayenne pepper

1lb. (450g) new potatoes, quartered

8oz. (225g) pancetta, prosciutto, or bacon slices, roughly chopped

12oz. (350g) peppery salad leaves, such as watercress, mustard leaf, and arugula, washed and dried

salt and freshly ground black pepper

1 Put the lemon zest and rosemary leaves into a large bowl with the vinegar, wine, garlic, oregano, and 4 tbsp. oil from the artichokes. Stir well. Using a fork, pierce the skin of the chickens in five or six places, then season well with ground black pepper and the cayenne pepper. Put the birds, breast-side down, in the bowl and spoon the marinade over them. Cover and chill overnight.

2 Boil the potatoes in salted water for 2 minutes. Drain. Heat the oven to 400°F (350°F convection oven).

3 Lift the birds from the marinade and place, breast-side up, in a large roasting pan. Scatter the potatoes, pancetta, and the artichokes around them, then pour the marinade over. Roast for 1½ hours, basting occasionally, or until golden and cooked through.

4 Cut each squab in half lengthwise and keep them warm. Toss the salad leaves with about 5 tbsp. of the warm cooking juices. Arrange the leaves on warm plates, then top with the potatoes, pancetta, artichokes, and the squab. Serve immediately.

SAVE MONEY

Use the oil drained from the artichokes to make a salad dressing.

Serves 6

Roast Duck with Orange Sauce

Prep time: 50 minutes
Cooking time: about 1¾ hours, plus resting

2 large oranges

2 large fresh thyme sprigs

5lb. (2.3kg) duck, preferably with the giblets

4 tbsp. vegetable oil

2 shallots, chopped

1 tsp. all-purpose flour

2½ cups (600ml) chicken stock (see page 155)

2 tbsp. sugar

2 tbsp. red wine vinegar

7 tbsp. fresh orange juice

7 tbsp. fruity German white wine, such as Riesling

2 tbsp. orange liqueur, such as Grand Marnier (optional)

1 tbsp. lemon juice

salt and freshly ground black pepper

fresh mint and Glazed Orange Wedges (see opposite) to garnish

snow peas and broccoli to serve

1   Heat the oven to 400°F (350°F convection oven). Using a zester, remove strips from the oranges. Put half the zest into a pan of cold water and bring to a boil, then drain and put to one side. Remove the pith from both oranges, then cut the flesh into segments.

2   Put the thyme and unblanched orange zest inside the duck, then season. Rub the skin with 2 tbsp. of the oil and sprinkle with salt. Place, breast-side up, on a rack over a roasting pan. Roast for 30 minutes, basting after 20 minutes, then turn the bird breast-side down and roast for about 35 minutes, basting again after 20 minutes. Turn the bird breast-side up and roast for 10 minutes longer, or until just cooked through and the juices run clear when the thickest part of the thigh is pierced with a skewer. If there are any traces of pink in the juice, put the bird back into the oven and roast for 10 minutes, then check again.

3   Meanwhile, cut the gizzard, heart, and neck into pieces. Heat the

remaining 2 tbsp. oil in a heavy-bottomed pan, add the giblets, and fry until dark brown. Add the shallots and flour and cook for 1 minute. Pour in the stock, bring to a boil, and bubble until it reduces by half; strain.

4 Put the sugar and vinegar into another pan over low heat and stir until the sugar dissolves. Increase the heat and cook until it forms a dark caramel. Pour in the orange juice and stir. Cool, cover, and put to one side.

5 Lift the duck off the rack and keep it warm. Tilt the roasting pan and skim all the fat off the juices to leave about 3 tbsp. sediment. Stir the wine into the sediment, then put the pan over medium heat on the stovetop, bring to a boil, and bubble for 5 minutes, or until syrupy. Add the stock mixture and orange mixture and bring back to a boil, then bubble until syrupy, skimming if necessary. To serve the sauce, add the blanched orange zest and segments. Add the orange liqueur, if you like, and lemon juice to taste.

6 Carve the duck and garnish with mint and glazed orange wedges. Serve with the orange sauce, snow peas, and broccoli.

Serves 4

Glazed Orange Wedges

To glaze oranges, quarter them or cut into wedges, dust with a little superfine sugar, and broil until caramelized.

Roast Guinea Fowl

Prep time: 20 minutes, plus marinating
Cooking time: 1¼ hours, plus resting

1 oven-ready guinea fowl

2 lemons—grated zest and juice of one, one quartered lengthwise

3 bay leaves

5 fresh thyme sprigs

1 tbsp. black peppercorns, lightly crushed

2 tbsp. butter

⅔ cup (160ml) hot chicken stock (see page 155)

roast potatoes and green beans to serve

For the gravy

2 tbsp. red currant jelly

7 tbsp. dry white wine

salt and freshly ground black pepper

1   Put the guinea fowl into a bowl and add the lemon zest and juice, bay leaves, thyme, and peppercorns. Cover and leave to marinate for 1 hour. Heat the oven to 400°F (350°F convection oven).

2   Put the bird into a roasting pan, breast-side down, then put the lemon quarters and butter into the cavity, pour the hot stock over, and roast for 50 minutes.

3   Turn the guinea fowl breast-side up and continue to roast for 20 minutes, or until cooked through and the juices run clear when the thigh is pierced with a skewer.

4   Transfer the guinea fowl to a board, cover loosely with foil, and leave to rest for 10 minutes.

5   To make the gravy, put the roasting pan on the stovetop over a low heat and scrape up the juices. Add the red currant jelly, wine, and 4 tbsp. water. Bring to a boil, then reduce the heat and simmer. stirring, for 3–5 minutes. Season well. Carve the guinea fowl and serve with the gravy, roast potatoes, and green beans.

Serves 4

Roast Grouse

🍴 **Prep time:** 10 minutes
Cooking time: 40 minutes, plus resting

2 oven-ready grouse
6 bacon slices
2 tbsp. vegetable oil
2 tbsp. freshly chopped rosemary or
    thyme (optional)
salt and freshly ground black pepper
Parsnip and Potato Chips (see below)
    or hand-cooked salted chips and
    watercress to serve

Parsnip and Potato Chips

Using a vegetable peeler, cut thin strips off each vegetable. Heat a saucepan half full of sunflower oil until a small cube of bread browns in 20 seconds. Fry the strips, a few at a time, until golden. Drain on paper towels and serve immediately.

1. Heat the oven to 400°F (350°F convection oven). Put the grouse into a large roasting pan, with enough space between them so that they can brown evenly. Cover the breast of each with bacon slices and drizzle with 1 tbsp. of the oil, then season with salt and ground black pepper. Sprinkle with herbs, if you like.
2. Roast for about 40 minutes until the juices run clear when the thigh is pierced with a skewer.
3. Transfer the grouse to a board, cover loosely with foil, and leave to rest for 10 minutes.
4. Serve with the Parsnip and Potato Chips, plus watercress to contrast with the richness of the meat.

Serves 4

Perfect Pork

Honey Pork with Roasted Potatoes and Apples

Prep time: 20 minutes
Cooking time: 1¾ hours, plus resting

2¼lb. (1kg) pork rib roast, with skin and
   four bones, at room temperature

4 tbsp. olive oil

2 tbsp. butter

1½lb. (700g) waxy salad potatoes,
   scrubbed and halved

1 large onion, cut into eight wedges

2 crisp dessert apples, such as Cox's

1 tbsp. honey mixed with 1 tbsp.
   wholegrain mustard

12 fresh sage leaves

¾ cup (175ml) hard cider

salt and freshly ground black pepper

1　Heat the oven to 475°F (425°F
convection oven). Put the pork on a
board and use a paring knife to score
the skin into thin strips, cutting about
halfway into the fat underneath. Rub
1 tsp. salt and 2 tbsp. of the oil over
the skin and season well with ground
black pepper. Put the meat on a rack,
skin-side up, over a large roasting
pan (or just put the pork in the pan).
Roast for 20 minutes. Reduce the
oven temperature to 375°F (325°F
convection oven) and continue to
roast for 15 minutes longer.

2　Add the remaining oil and the butter
to the roasting pan. Scatter the
potatoes and onion around the meat,
season with salt and black pepper,
and continue to roast for 45 minutes.

3　Meanwhile, core the apples and cut
each into six wedges. Take the roasting
pan out of the oven and brush the meat
with the honey and mustard mixture.
Add the apples and sage leaves to the
pan and roast for 15 minutes longer,
or until the pork is cooked through.

4　Remove the pork from the pan and
wrap completely with foil, then leave
to rest for 10 minutes. Turn down
the oven to 300°F (250°F convection
oven). Put the potatoes, onions, and
apples into a warm serving dish and

put back in the oven to keep warm.

5 Tilt the roasting pan and pour off as much of the fat as you can, leaving just the dark brown juices. Put the roasting pan on the stovetop over medium heat, add the cider, and stir well to make a thin gravy. Season.

6 Cut the meat away from the bone. Cut between each bone. Pull the crisp skin away from the meat and cut into strips. Carve the roast, giving each person some crisp skin and a bone to chew. Serve with the gravy and potatoes, onion, and apples.

Serves 4

Perfect Loin of Pork

Pork loin can be roasted on or off the bone. Tenderloin and center-cut pork loin roasts are popular boneless. Lean roasts and the impressive-looking rib roast have the extra flavor that comes from the rib bones. Take care not to overcook a roast or the meat will be dry and tough.

1. Trim away excess fat and sinews. Shape the stuffing into a thin sheet or cylinder. Lay the loin with the fat-side down on the cutting board and put the stuffing on the line where the eye of loin meets the flap meat. Fold the flap of meat over the eye and secure with skewers.
2. Tie the roast with string every 2in. (5cm) and remove the skewers.

Perfect crisp skin

- ❑ If possible, ask the butcher to score the skin for you.
- ❑ The pork skin needs to be dry. Remove any wrapping and pat the skin dry with paper towels.
- ❑ Leave the roast uncovered in the refrigerator overnight to dry out the skin.
- ❑ Use your sharpest knife or a razor blade to score the skin, cutting about halfway into the fat underneath.
- ❑ Rub the scored skin with a little olive oil and salt.

1

Pork roasting times

Heat the oven to 350°F (325°F convection oven).

Note Many cooks give pork an initial blast of heat—450°F (400°F convection oven) or even higher—for 15-20 minutes before reducing the temperature. If you do this, watch the roast carefully near the end of its cooking time.

OFF THE BONE	COOKING TIME PER 1LB. (450G)
Well done	25–30 minutes

ON THE BONE	COOKING TIME PER 1LB. (450G)
Well done	30–35 minutes

Use the times above as a guideline, but remember roasting times will vary depending on how the meat has been aged and stored, the shape and thickness of the roast, and personal taste. Ovens vary as well. If a recipe gives a different oven temperature, follow the recipe for timing.

How to tell if pork is cooked

To check if pork is cooked, pierce the thickest part of the meat with a skewer. The juices that run out should be golden and clear. If there are any traces of pink in the juice, put back into the oven and roast for 10–15 minutes longer, then check again in the same way.

Resting

When the pork is cooked, cover loosely with foil and leave to rest for 30 minutes before carving. Larger roasts can rest for up to 45 minutes without getting cold.

Carving pork with crisp skin

1   It is much easier to slice pork if you first remove the crisp skin. Remove any string and position the carving knife just under the skin on the topmost side of the roast. Work the knife under the skin, taking care not to cut into the meat, until you can pull it off with your fingers.

2   Slice the meat, then snap the skin into pieces for serving.

Crisp Roasted Pork with Applesauce

Prep time: 30 minutes, plus standing
Cooking time: about 2¼ hours, plus resting

3½lb. (1.6kg) boneless pork loin roast, with skin

olive oil

2¼lb. (1kg) cooking apples, cored and roughly chopped

1–2 tbsp. sugar

1 tbsp. all-purpose flour

2½ cups (600ml) chicken stock (see page 155), hard cider or apple juice

salt and freshly ground black pepper

new potatoes and green vegetables to serve

1 Score the pork skin, sprinkle generously with salt, and leave at room temperature for 1–2 hours.

2 Heat the oven to 425°F (400°F convection oven). Wipe the salt off the skin, rub with oil, and sprinkle again with salt. Put half the apples into a small roasting pan, sit the pork on top, and roast for 30 minutes.

Reduce the oven temperature to 375°F (325°F convection oven) and roast for 1½ hours longer, or until cooked through.

3 Meanwhile, put the remaining apples into a pan with the sugar and 2 tbsp. water, cover with a tight-fitting lid, and cook until just soft. Set aside.

4 Transfer the pork to a serving dish, cover loosely with foil, and leave to rest while you make the gravy. Skim off most of the fat in the pan, leaving about 1 tbsp. and the apples. Put the pan on the stovetop over medium heat. Stir in the flour until smooth, then stir in the stock or cider and bring to a boil. Bubble slowly for 2–3 minutes, skimming if necessary. Strain the sauce through a strainer into a serving bowl, pushing through as much of the apple as possible. Slice the pork and serve with the sauce, new potatoes, and green vegetables.

Serves 6

Roast Pork with Fennel

Prep time: 25 minutes
Cooking time: about 1½ hours, plus resting

4 fresh rosemary sprigs

6 large garlic cloves

3 tsp. fennel seeds

3½lb. (1.6kg) unrolled boneless pork loin roast, at room temperature

1¼ cups (300 ml) dry white wine

salt and freshly ground black pepper

mashed potatoes and curly kale to serve

1   Heat the oven to 425°F (400°F convection oven). Set aside two rosemary sprigs, then strip the leaves off the remainder. Put the garlic, rosemary leaves, fennel seeds, 1 tsp. salt, and 1 tsp. black pepper into a food processor and mix to a smooth paste.

2   Score the fat side of the pork with a sharp knife, then rub the flesh side with the garlic and rosemary paste.

Rub salt over the fat side. Roll up the loin, then tie along its length at 1in. (2.5cm) intervals with kitchen string. Weigh the roast and calculate the cooking time, allowing 25 minutes per 1lb. (450g).

3   Heat a roasting pan on the stovetop and brown the pork all over, then add the wine and remaining rosemary sprigs. Put into the oven and roast for 20 minutes, then reduce the oven temperature to 400°F (350°F convection oven) and roast for the remaining calculated time.

4   Transfer the meat to a board, cover loosely with foil, and leave to rest for 15 minutes. Slice the pork and serve with the pan juices poured over, with mashed potatoes and curly kale.

Serves 6

Cider Roasted Pork

Prep time: 10 minutes, plus marinating
Cooking time: about 1½ hours, plus resting

2½lb. (1.1kg) rolled boneless pork loin
   roast, fat removed

1 tbsp. olive oil

2 red onions, quartered

2 apples, cored and quartered

a few fresh thyme sprigs, chopped

2 cups (450ml) hard cider or apple juice

salt and freshly ground black pepper

cabbage to serve

1   Put the pork into a bowl, then add the oil, onions, apples, and thyme. Pour in the cider, cover, and marinate in the refrigerator for 4 hours, or overnight.

2   Take the pork out of the refrigerator 1 hour before roasting to let it return to room temperature. Heat the oven to 400°F (350°F convection oven). Put the pork into a roasting pan with the marinade ingredients and season. Roast for about 1½ hours until the pork is cooked through. Remove the pork from the pan, cover with foil and leave to rest.

3   To make the cider gravy, drain the roasting juices into a pan, bring to a boil, and bubble for 5 minutes, or until they reduce and thicken. Slice the pork and serve with the gravy and cabbage.

Serves 4

Wrapped Pork and Sage

Prep time: 15 minutes
Cooking time: about 30 minutes, plus resting

14oz. (400g) rolled puff pastry dough

1 large egg, beaten

3oz. (75g) pancetta slices

2 × 14-oz. (400g) pieces pork tenderloin, even thickness, membrane removed

1 tbsp. freshly chopped sage

freshly ground black pepper

Roasted Baby Potatoes (see page 146), Spiced Red Cabbage (see page 148), and Applesauce (see page 164) to serve

1   Heat the oven to 425°F (375°F convection oven). Unroll the pastry dough and cut out a 4½ × 11in. (11.5 × 28cm) rectangle. Transfer to a cookie sheet and brush with some of the egg.

2   Arrange the pancetta slices side-by-side on a board, overlapping them a little. Lay one of the pork tenderloins horizontally across the middle of the pancetta slices. Press the sage on top of the pork, then season well with ground black pepper. Top with the second pork tenderloin.

3   Fold the pancetta around the pork and put the wrapped tenderloin, seam-side down, on top of the dough. Cut ¼in. (0.5cm) wide strips from the remaining dough, each long enough to cover the tenderloins. Arrange the strips in a crisscross pattern over the pork, pressing the ends of the strips to the bottom to help them stick. Brush with the rest of the beaten egg.

4   Roast the pork package for about 25–30 minutes until the pastry is dark golden. Transfer to a board, cover with foil, and leave to rest for 10 minutes.

5   Serve in slices with Roasted Baby Potatoes, Spiced Red Cabbage, and some Applesauce.

SAVE TIME

Prepare the wrapped pork to the end of step 3 up to 3 hours ahead. Chill. Complete step 4 to serve, roasting for 30–35 minutes.

SAVE MONEY

A stack of pork tenderloins makes a relatively inexpensive, quick, and meltingly tender roast.

Serves 6

Stuffed Rack of Pork with Cider Gravy

Prep time: 30 minutes
Cooking time: about 2 hours, plus resting

14oz. (400g) apple-flavored pork sausage
   meat

a large handful of fresh parsley,
   finely chopped

finely grated zest of 1 lemon

2 tbsp. wholegrain mustard

4½lb. (2kg) rack of pork at room
   temperature

2 onions, sliced in thick rings

salt and freshly ground black pepper

For the gravy

2 tbsp. all-purpose flour

¾ cup + 2 tbsp. (200ml) hard cider, apple
   cider, or apple juice

2 cups (450ml) chicken stock
   (see page 155)

1 tbsp. honey or red currant jelly

½ tbsp. wholegrain mustard

1   Heat the oven to 425°F (400°F convection oven). Put the sausage meat into a bowl and mix in the parsley, lemon zest, mustard, and some ground black pepper. (The sausage meat should provide enough salt.)

2   Make a "flap" along the length of the meat by partially cutting the skin and fat away from the meat. Press the sausage mixture into this space, then tie the skin flap in place with string around the roast, all along its length. Weigh the joint and calculate the cooking time, allowing 25 minutes per 1lb. (450g).

3   Keeping the onion rings intact, place them in the bottom of a roasting pan just large enough to hold the meat. Rest the pork on top, skin-side up.

4   Season the skin with salt and roast for the calculated time, reducing the oven temperature to 350°F (325°F convection oven) after the first 40 minutes. Continue roasting for the calculated time, or until the juices run clear when the meat is pierced deeply with a knife. If using a meat thermometer, the temperature should hit 158°F in the thickest part of the roast.

5   Transfer the pork to a board and cover loosely with foil. Leave to rest in a warm place for at least 30 minutes while you make the gravy.

6   Tilt the roasting pan and spoon off all but 1 tbsp. of the fat. Put the pan on the stovetop over medium heat, sprinkle in the flour, and stir, scraping up all the meaty bits stuck to the bottom. Take the pan off the heat and gradually stir in the cider. Put the pan back onto the heat and bubble for 2 minutes, stirring often. Add the stock and bring to a boil, then reduce the heat and simmer for 15 minutes, or until the gravy reaches the desired consistency.

7   Strain the gravy into a warm gravy boat—or into a clean pan to reheat later—and stir in the honey or red currant jelly, the mustard, and any juices that have leaked from the pork. Check the seasoning. Serve immediately with the meat, or put to one side for reheating later.

57

SAVE TIME

Prepare the pork to the end of step 3 up to one day ahead. Cover and chill. To roast, let it to come to room temperature, then dry the skin with paper towels before roasting, then complete steps 4, 5, 6, and 7 to finish the recipe.

SAVE EFFORT

The meat can be left to rest for up to 1 hour before carving. If the crisp skin softens under the foil, crisp it again under a hot broiler.

Here's a stress-free technique to avoid feeling pressured when making gravy just before serving: transfer the roast to a clean roasting pan 30 minutes before the end of the calculated time, then continue roasting in the new pan. Use the juices in the original pan to make gravy while the roast finishes roasting.

An easy way to carve this roast is to first remove the bones all at once by slicing down just above them. Then simply slice the meat.

Serves 8–10

Perfect Roasted Pork Belly

Prep time: 15 minutes, plus drying
Cooking time: about 3½ hours, plus resting

3¼-lb. (1.5kg) piece of pork belly
salt

1 Using a small, sharp knife, score lines into the pork skin (cutting into the fat) about ½in. (1cm) apart, but not so deep that you cut into the meat. Pat the pork completely dry, then leave uncovered at room temperature to air dry for about 45 minutes.

2 Heat the oven to 425°F (400°F convection). Rub lots of salt over the pork skin. Rest a wire rack above a deep roasting pan and put the pork, skin-side up, on the rack. Roast for 30 minutes, then reduce the oven temperature to 325°F (300°F convection oven) and continue roasting for 3 hours longer—by this stage the skin should be crisp and golden. (If not, don't panic—see Save Effort, right).

3 Transfer the pork to a board and use a sharp knife to slice off the skin in one piece (about the outer ¾in./2cm). Cover the pork meat loosely with foil and leave to rest for 30–40 minutes.

4 Cut the crisp skin into six long strips, then cut the pork belly into six equal portions. Serve each portion topped with a strip of the skin.

SAVE EFFORT

If the skin isn't as crisp as you'd like, you can still rescue it. Remove the skin as above and heat the broiler to medium-high. Put the whole piece of skin on a cookie sheet and broil until crisp and puffed. Watch carefully to avoid scorching, turning the cookie sheet to avoid any hot spots. Complete the recipe as above to serve.

Serves 6

Perfect Ham

Hams come from the hind legs of hogs. They are sold fresh, brined, or smoked, and come in various sizes. Hams labeled as "ready to eat" are exactly that, but others, such as the premium Virginia Smithfield hams, require cooking before serving.

Preparing and roasting ham

1   If a ham needs to be soaked, place it in a large container that will hold it comfortably with plenty of space for water. Pour cold water over it to cover and weigh down the ham, if necessary. Leave to soak overnight, then drain well.

2   Put the ham into a large Dutch oven and cover with fresh cold water. Add a few sprigs of parsley, a few peppercorns, a bay leaf, and a chopped onion to the water, if you like. Bring to just below boiling point—do not let the water boil or the meat will be tough. Skim off any surface scum. Simmer gently for 25 minutes per 1lb. (450g), checking occasionally to make sure the meat remains covered with water.

1

4

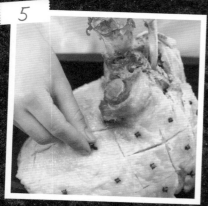

5

6

3　Leave to cool in the water. Transfer the ham to a roasting pan. (Put the broth to one side for soup.)

4　Heat the oven to 400°F (350°F convection oven). Remove the rind and neatly trim the fat so there is a ¼–½in. (0.5–1cm) layer left on the meat.

5　Score the fat with parallel lines about 2in. (5cm) apart, then score on the diagonal to make diamond shapes. Press a clove into the middle of each diamond.

6　Spread prepared English mustard thinly and evenly over the ham —or glaze as the recipe suggests. Sprinkle with soft brown sugar to make a light but even coating. Bake the ham for about 30 minutes until golden brown.

Quick Roasted Ham

Pressure Cooker Recipe

Prep time: 20 minutes
Cooking time: about 40 minutes

2¼lb. (1kg) unsmoked, boneless fresh ham roast

6 whole allspice berries

2–3 sprigs each fresh thyme and parsley

6 black peppercorns

8oz. (225g) baby carrots

8oz. (225g) baby leeks

8oz. (225g) baby parsnips, halved

8oz. (225g) shallots, halved if large

2 small green cabbages (total weight about 1lb./450g), quartered

3 tbsp. wholegrain mustard

3 tbsp. honey

3 tbsp. olive oil

salt and freshly ground black pepper

1   Put the ham into a pressure cooker. Pour in enough water to half-fill the pan, then add the allspice, thyme, parsley, and peppercorns. Cover, put to the highest setting, and bring up to pressure. Following the manufacturer's directions, cook for 25 minutes. If your pressure cooker doesn't have a steam quick-release system, run the cold water in the sink and hold the pan underneath it to reduce the pressure quickly. Lift out the ham, then cover and set aside.

2   Bring the stock back to a boil. Add the carrots, leeks, parsnips, shallots, and cabbages, and blanch for 2 minutes. Drain well, discarding the stock.

3   Heat the oven to 475°F (425°F convection oven). Put the ham into a roasting pan along with the blanched vegetables. Mix the mustard with the honey and 1 tbsp. of the oil and drizzle over the ham. Pour the rest of the oil over the vegetables and season them. Roast for 10–15 minutes until golden. Slice the ham and serve hot with the vegetables.

SAVE MONEY

Instead of discarding the stock at step 2, chill or freeze it. You can then use to make soup.

Serves 4

Maple-, Ginger-, and Soy-roasted Ham

Prep time: 10 minutes, plus soaking (optional)
Cooking time: about 2¼ hours

2 × 5½lb. (2.5kg) smoked, boneless
  fresh hams

8 tbsp. vegetable oil

3in. (7.5cm) piece of ginger root, peeled
  and grated

8 tbsp. maple syrup

6 tbsp. dark soy sauce

12 star anise (optional)

1 If the ham is salty (check with your
   butcher or the label), soak it in cold
   water overnight. Alternatively, put
   it in a large pan of water and bring
   to a boil. Reduce the heat and simmer
   for 10 minutes, then drain.

2 Heat the oven to 400°F (350°F
   convection oven). Put the roasts into
   a large roasting pan and pour 4 tbsp.
   of the oil over them. Cover with foil
   and roast for 1 hour 50 minutes, or for
   20 minutes per 1lb. (450g).

3 Mix the ginger, maple syrup, soy
   sauce, and the remaining oil together.

4 Take the ham out of the oven, remove
   the foil, and leave to cool a little, then
   carefully peel away the skin and
   discard. Score the fat in a crisscross
   pattern, stud with the star anise, if
   using, then pour the ginger sauce
   over. Return to the oven and roast for
   20 minutes longer, or until the glaze
   is golden brown. Slice and serve one
   joint warm. Cool the other, wrap in
   foil, and chill until needed.

SAVE EFFORT

Home-cooked ham is great hot
or cold, but cooking a single large
ham is often impractical. Roasting
two medium hams at the same time
means you can serve one hot and
still have plenty left to eat cold.

Perfect Lamb

Roast Lamb and Boulangère Potatoes

Prep time: 25 minutes
Cooking time: about 1½ hours, plus resting

4½lb. (2kg) Idaho or other baking potatoes, thinly sliced into circles—a mandoline is ideal for this

1 large onion, thinly sliced

10 fresh thyme sprigs

1¾ cups (400ml) hot chicken stock (see page 155)

2 chamomile tea bags

2 tsp. sunflower oil

3½lb. (1.6kg) lamb bone-in shoulder roast at room temperature

salt and freshly ground black pepper

mint sauce or red currant jelly and seasonal vegetables to serve

1   Heat the oven to 400°F (350°F convection oven). Layer the potato slices, onion, and half the thyme in a large baking dish suitable for serving from, seasoning as you go. Pour the hot stock over. Put a large wire rack over the dish.

2   Empty the contents of the chamomile tea bags into a small bowl (discard the bags). Stir in the leaves from the remaining thyme, some seasoning, and the oil. Rub the chamomile mixture over the lamb. Sit the lamb on the wire rack on top of the dish. Cover everything with foil.

3   Carefully transfer the dish to the oven and roast for 1 hour. Uncover and roast for 30 minutes longer (the lamb should be cooked to medium), or until the lamb is cooked to your liking and the potatoes are tender and golden.

4   Transfer the lamb to a board, cover with foil, and leave to rest for 20 minutes; keep the potatoes warm in the oven. Serve the lamb and potatoes with mint sauce or red currant jelly and seasonal vegetables.

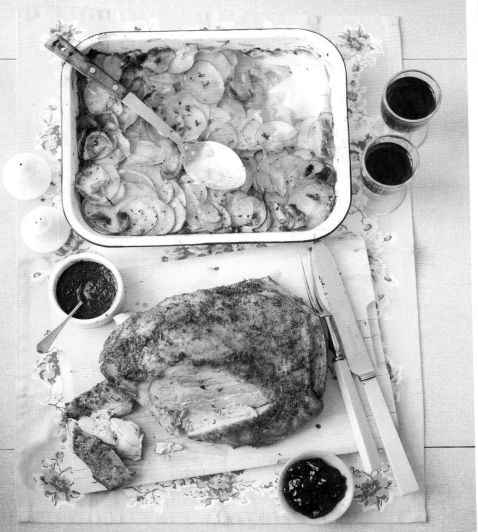

Serves 8

Slow-Roasted Lamb Shoulder

Prep time: 20 minutes
Cooking time: about 4 hours 10 minutes, plus resting

4 canned anchovy fillets, chopped

finely grated zest of 1 lemon

3 fresh rosemary sprigs, leaves picked
   and chopped

2 tbsp. olive oil

4½lb. (2kg) bone-in lamb shoulder roast
   at room temperature

1 large onion, unpeeled and cut into
   thick rings

5 unpeeled garlic cloves

salt and freshly ground black pepper

For the gravy

2 tbsp. cornstarch

7 tbsp. dry white wine

a small handful of fresh mint

1 Heat the oven to 425°F (400°F
   convection oven). Put the anchovy
   fillets, lemon zest, rosemary, oil, and
   plenty of seasoning into a small bowl
   and mix well. Next, lay the lamb
   shoulder on a board and slash the fatty
   side well with a sharp knife. Rub the
   marinade all over the lamb.

2 Put the onion and garlic into a roasting
   pan just large enough to hold the lamb.
   Lay the lamb on top, slashed-side up,
   and cover the pan with foil. Reduce
   the oven temperature to 325°F (300°F
   convection oven). Slow-roast for 4 hours,
   removing the foil for the last 45 minutes
   to let the lamb brown. The lamb is ready
   when you can easily shred the meat off
   the bone with two forks.

3 Transfer the lamb to a board and cover
   again with foil while you make the
   gravy—the lamb can rest for up to 45
   minutes.

4 Tilt the roasting pan and pour off most
   of the fat, leaving the onion and garlic
   in the pan. Whisk in the cornstarch,
   then the wine and mint (stems and all).
   Bring to a boil, whisking frequently
   and squishing the vegetables until the
   gravy thickens. Add about 7 tbsp. water
   and simmer until the gravy reaches the
   desired consistency. Strain, then taste
   and check the seasoning. Serve with
   the shredded lamb.

Serves 8

Herbed Crown Roast of Lamb

Prep time: 10 minutes
Cooking time: about 35 minutes, plus resting

1¾lb. (800g) 16-bone crown roast of lamb at room temperature

2 tbsp. olive oil

5 fresh thyme sprigs, leaves removed

¾oz. (20g) fresh flat-leaf parsley

1 large garlic clove, roughly chopped

1 tbsp. Dijon mustard

salt and freshly ground black pepper

1 Heat the oven to 400°F (350°F convection oven). Put the lamb crown roast on a baking sheet. Put the remaining ingredients and plenty of salt and ground black pepper into a blender (or use a mortar and pestle) and blend (or mash together) until well combined.

2 Rub the herb mixture over the lamb, then roast for 30–35 minutes for pink meat (roast longer if you like meat more well done). Transfer the lamb to a board. Cover loosely with a few layers of foil and leave to rest for 20–30 minutes.

3 To serve, slice the crown into 16 chops by cutting between the bones.

SAVE TIME

Rub the herb mixture over the lamb up to 3 hours ahead, then chill. Take the lamb out of the refrigerator 40 minutes before roasting so it returns to room temperature, then complete the recipe.

SAVE EFFORT

Remember to order the crown roast in advance from a butcher so they have time to prepare it for you.

Perfect Roast Lamb

From tender juicy noisettes of tenderloin to boned or butterflied leg for roasting, a rack tied in the French style or prepared as an elegant guard of honor, lamb is wonderfully versatile, and often under-appreciated.

Heat the oven to 425°F (400°F convection oven). Weigh the roast to calculate the roasting time. Brown the lamb in the hot oven for 20 minutes, then reduce the oven temperature to 375°F (325°F convection oven) and roast for the calculated time.

	COOKING TIME PER 1LB. (450G)
Medium	15–20 minutes
Well done	20–25 minutes

Use these times as a guideline, but remember roasting times will vary depending on how the meat has been aged and stored, the shape and thickness of the roast, and personal taste. Ovens vary as well. If a recipe gives a different oven temperature, follow the recipe for timing.

How to tell if lamb is cooked

To check if roast lamb is cooked as you like it, insert a thin skewer into the middle and press out some juices: the pinker the juice that runs out, the rarer the meat.

Resting

When the lamb is cooked, cover loosely with foil and leave to rest for 20 minutes before carving. Larger roasts can rest for up to 45 minutes without getting cold.

Carving leg of lamb

There are two ways to carve a leg of lamb. The first gives slices with a section of the crust; the second starts with slices that are well done and then get progressively rarer.

Leg of lamb: method 1

1 Hold the shank and cut from that end, holding the knife flat on the bone, a couple of inches into the meat. Cut down onto the bone to remove that chunk and slice thinly.

2 Start cutting thin slices from the meat on the bone, starting at the cut left by the chunk you removed. Hold the knife at right angles to the bone, then cut at a slight angle as you reach the thicker sections of meat.

3 When you have taken off all the meat you can on that side, turn the leg round and continue slicing at an angle until all the meat is removed.

Leg of lamb: method 2

1 Hold the shank with the meatiest part of the leg facing up. Slice with the knife blade parallel to the bone. When you reach the bone, turn the leg over and continue slicing (knife blade parallel to the bone) until you reach the bone.

2 Remove the remainder of the meat from both sides in single pieces and slice thinly.

1

2

Roast Spiced Leg of Lamb

Prep time: 25 minutes, plus minimum overnight and up to 24 hours marinating
Cooking time: 2¼ hours

3½–4lb. (1.6–1.8kg) leg of lamb

2 tbsp. each cumin seeds and coriander seeds

½ cup blanched or slivered almonds

1 onion, chopped

6 garlic cloves, roughly chopped

1in. (2.5cm) piece of ginger root, peeled and grated

4 hot green chilies, seeded and chopped (see Safety Tip, opposite)

2 cups plain yogurt

½ tsp. each cayenne pepper and garam masala

3½ tsp. salt

4 tbsp. vegetable oil

½ tsp. whole cloves, 16 cardamom pods, 1 cinnamon stick, 10 black peppercorns

flat-leaf parsley sprigs to garnish

1 Put the lamb into a large, shallow nonmetallic dish and put to one side. Put the cumin and coriander seeds into a pan and cook over high heat until aromatic. Grind to a fine powder in a mortar and pestle, or use a spice grinder. Put to one side.

2 Put the almonds, onion, garlic, ginger, chilies, and 3 tbsp. of the yogurt into a food processor and blend to a paste. Put the remaining yogurt into a bowl, stir well and add the paste, ground cumin and coriander, cayenne pepper, garam masala, and salt. Stir well.

3 Spoon the yogurt mixture over the lamb and use a brush to push it into all the nooks and crannies. Turn the lamb, making sure it is well coated, then cover and leave to marinate in the refrigerator for 24 hours.

4 Take the lamb out of the refrigerator 1 hour before roasting so it returns to room temperature. Heat the oven to 400°F (350°F convection oven). Put the lamb and marinade into a roasting pan. Heat the oil in a small skillet, add the whole spices and fry until they are aromatic. Pour over the lamb. Cover the roasting pan with foil

and roast for 1½ hours. Uncover and continue roasting the lamb for 45 minutes longer, basting occasionally.

5 Transfer the lamb to a serving dish. Pick the spices out of the pan to use as a garnish. Press the sauce through a fine strainer into a bowl. Garnish the lamb with the spices and parsley, and serve the sauce on the side.

Serves 6

Roast Leg of Lamb with Rosemary

Prep time: 15 minutes
Cooking time: 1½ hours, plus resting

5½lb. (2.5kg) leg of lamb

4 fresh rosemary sprigs

1½ tsp. oil

4 garlic cloves, cut into slivers

4 canned anchovy fillets, roughly chopped

4 fresh oregano sprigs

1 large onion, thickly sliced

1 lemon, cut into 6 wedges

salt and freshly ground black pepper

vegetables to serve

1   Take the lamb out of the refrigerator 1 hour in advance. Pat the skin dry.

2   Heat the oven to 425°F (400°F convection oven). Cut the rosemary into smaller sprigs. Rub the oil over the lamb. Cut small slits all over the meat, then insert the garlic slivers, rosemary sprigs, anchovy pieces, and the leaves from two oregano sprigs into the gaps. Season well.

3   Put the onion slices into the bottom of a roasting pan just large enough to hold the lamb. Top with the remaining oregano, then put in the meat, fat-side up. (The onions must be covered to prevent them burning.) Tuck lemon wedges around the meat.

4   Put the lamb into the oven and reduce the oven temperature to 375°F (325°F convection oven). Roast for 15 minutes per 1lb. (450g) for pink meat, or longer if you like it more well done.

5   Transfer the lamb to a board, cover with foil, and leave to rest for 30 minutes before carving. Carefully pour (or skim) off the fat from a corner of the roasting pan, leaving the sediment behind. Put the pan on the stovetop over medium heat and pour in 1¼–2 cups (300–450ml) vegetable water (or meat stock). Stir thoroughly, scraping up the sediment, and boil steadily until the gravy is a rich brown color. Serve the lamb with the gravy and vegetables.

SAVE TIME

Prepare the lamb to the end of step 3 up to 2 hours ahead. When ready to cook, complete the recipe. The lamb is served pink here, but allow an extra 20–30 minutes if you prefer your meat more well done.

Serves 8

Roast Lamb with Harissa

Prep time: 40 minutes
Cooking time: about 2 hours, plus resting

4lb. (1.8kg) boned leg of lamb, plus
　bones, at room temperature

2 tbsp. olive oil

1 bunch of fresh rosemary

1 bunch of fresh thyme

2 cups shallots, peeled, roots left intact,
　and blanched

1 head of garlic, broken up into cloves,
　skin left on

1¼ cups (300ml) dry white wine

2½ cups (600ml) lamb or chicken stock
　(see page 155)

salt and freshly ground black pepper

broiled chilies to garnish (optional)

couscous sprinkled with freshly
　chopped cilantro to serve

For the harissa

2 large red bell peppers (total weight
　about 14oz./400g)

4 large fresh red chilies, seeded and
　roughly chopped (see Safety Tip,
　page 79)

6 garlic cloves

1 tbsp. each ground coriander and
　caraway seeds

2 tsp. salt

4 tbsp. olive oil

1　To make the harissa, turn on the
broiler. Broil the peppers until the
skins are completely blackened and
the flesh is soft, then cover and leave
to cool. Peel off the skins, then
remove the cores and seeds. Put the
chilies into a food processor with the
garlic, ground coriander, and caraway
seeds, and blend to a paste. Add the
bell peppers, salt, and oil, and blend
for 1–2 minutes until smooth.

2　To prepare the lamb, spread the
bone cavity with about 3 tbsp. of the
harissa. Roll and secure with cocktail
picks, or sew up using a trussing
needle and thread.

3　Heat the oven to 400°F (350°F
convection oven). Heat the oil in a
roasting pan on the stovetop and
brown the lamb on all sides. Season,

place the rosemary and thyme under the lamb and add the bones to the roasting pan. Roast for 1 hour for pink lamb or 1½ hours for well done. Baste from time to time and add the shallots and garlic to the roasting pan 45 minutes before the end of the cooking time.

4   Transfer the lamb to a carving plate with the shallots and garlic. Cover loosely with foil and leave to rest in the oven at a low temperature.

5   Tilt the roasting pan and skim off any fat. Put the pan on the stovetop over medium heat. Add the wine, bring to a boil, and bubble until it reduces by half. Add the stock, return to a boil again, and continue bubbling until it reduces by half. Season, then strain.

6   Remove the cocktail picks or thread from the lamb and slice. Garnish with chilies, if you like. Serve with the shallots, garlic, gravy, and couscous.

Serves 6

How to Butterfly a Leg of Lamb

Removing the bone makes a tender, easy-to-carve roast.

1   Place the leg of lamb on a board with the meaty side facing down and the bone facing up. With the thick end facing toward you, see if the chunky end of the pelvic bone is in place. If it is, cut it out by working all around it with a boning knife—always cutting toward the bone—then pull or twist it out.

2   Cut a long slit right down to the bone, starting from the thin end, until you reach the joint. Scrape and cut the meat from the bone, pulling it back with your fingers, until the bone is fully exposed.

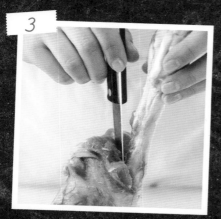

3

3 Work the knife carefully around the bone, cutting away from the meat, to loosen it. Twist out the bone, then follow the same procedure with the other bone.

4 Flatten the meat with your hands. Holding one hand flat on the top of the thickest part, make a cut parallel with the cutting board about midway through. Cut to within 1in. (2.5cm) of the edge, then fold the meat out as if opening a book. Repeat with the other thick part of the leg and fold out.

Butterflied Lamb with Garlic, Lemon, and Thyme

Prep time: 20 minutes, plus overnight marinating
Cooking time: about 1½ hours, plus resting

5lb. (2.3kg) leg of lamb, boned and
  butterflied (see page 84)
¾ cup (175ml) extra virgin olive oil, plus
  extra to brush
1 tbsp. dried oregano
3 tbsp. fresh thyme leaves
2 tbsp. freshly chopped flat-leaf parsley
6 garlic cloves, finely chopped
⅔ cup (160ml) balsamic vinegar
grated zest and juice of 2 small lemons
roast potatoes and green vegetables,
  or cherry tomatoes and a mixed-leaf
  salad, to serve

1 Open out the meat, lay skin-side
   down, and trim away any excess
   fat. Make slits all over it to help the
   marinade penetrate the flesh. Put
   the lamb into a non-metallic dish
   large enough to hold it flat. Whisk
   the oil, herbs, garlic, vinegar, and
   lemon zest and juice together

in a small bowl, and pour over
the meat, rubbing well into the
slits. Cover and leave to marinate
overnight in the refrigerator.

2 Remove the lamb from the
   refrigerator 1 hour before cooking
   to return to room temperature. Heat
   the oven to 425°F (400°F convection
   oven). Lift the lamb from the
   marinade (putting the marinade to
   one side) and roast for 20 minutes,
   then reduce the oven temperature
   to 375°F (325°F convection oven)
   and roast for 1 hour 10 minutes
   longer, basting with the marinade
   occasionally, or until the meat is
   cooked but still slightly pink in the
   middle.

3 Transfer the lamb to a board and
   cover loosely with foil. Leave to rest
   for 10 minutes before carving. Serve
   with potatoes and vegetables,
   or cherry tomatoes and a salad.

Serves 8

Perfect Rack of Lamb

A rack of lamb can contain up to nine ribs—chops from the neck end—served as a roast. Other names for rack of lamb are rack roast or rib roa[st]. Many butchers and supermarkets sell it with the bones already trimmed, a French-style rack, but if you need to trim the bones yourself, here's ho[w]

1. If necessary, pull off the papery outer membrane from the fat side of the rack. Trim away the excess fat. Look for a long strip of cartilage on one end of the rack and cut it out if it is there. Do the same with a long strip of sinew running the length of the rack under the ribs.

2. Make a cut right down to the bone across the fat side of the rack 1–2in. (2.5–5cm) from the tips of the bones. Place the knife in that cut and, holding the knife almost parallel to the ribs, slice off the meat as a single piece to expose the ends of the bones.

3

4

3   Insert the knife between one pair of bared ribs at the point of the initial cut. Push through it to cut away the meat between the ribs. Continue in the same way with the other ribs.

4   Slice down on both sides of each rib to remove the strips of meat. When you've finished, turn the rack bone-side up and scrape off the papery membranes from the backs of the ribs. This will leave the top parts of the bones clean.

Roasting a rack of lamb

A rack of lamb should always be cooked at a fairly high temperature so it browns well without overcooking the tender meat. Heat the oven to 425°F (400°F convection oven), then roast for 25–30 minutes. If you are cooking a single rack, an alternative is to brown the fat side first; this means that you can roast it at a lower temperature, 350°F (325°F convection oven).

Rack of Lamb with Balsamic Gravy

Prep time: 5 minutes
Cooking time: about 45 minutes, plus resting

4 fat garlic cloves, crushed

2 tbsp. herbes de Provence

6 tbsp. balsamic vinegar

¾ cup (175ml) olive oil

4 racks of lamb, excess fat trimmed off

salt and freshly ground black pepper

1　Heat the oven to 425°F (400°F convection oven). Put the garlic into a bowl with the herbs, 2 tbsp. of the vinegar, and 4 tbsp. of the oil. Season with salt and ground black pepper.

2　Put the lamb into a roasting pan and rub the garlic mixture into both the fat and meat. Roast for 25–30 minutes if you like the meat pink, or roast for 5–10 minutes longer if you like it well done. Transfer the lamb to a warm serving dish, cover loosely with foil, and leave to rest for 10 minutes.

3　Put the roasting pan on the stovetop over medium heat and whisk in the remaining vinegar and oil, scraping up any sediment as the liquid bubbles. Pour the gravy into a gravy boat or a bowl.

4　Slice the lamb into chops and serve with the gravy.

Serves 8

Couscous-Crusted Lamb

Prep time: 15 minutes
Cooking time: about 20 minutes, plus resting

scant ½ cup couscous

3 racks of lamb, excess fat trimmed off

2 tbsp. each dried cranberries, finely
chopped

2 tbsp. pistachios, finely chopped

2 large eggs

1½ tsp. wholegrain mustard

1½ tsp. dried mint

salt and freshly ground black pepper

1 Put the couscous into a bowl and
   pour ½ cup (125ml) boiling water
   over. Cover with plastic wrap and
   leave for 10 minutes.

2 Meanwhile, pat the lamb racks dry
   and put onto a baking sheet.

3 Heat the oven to 400°F (350°F
   convection oven). Use a fork to
   fluff the couscous, then stir in
   the cranberries, pistachios, eggs,
   mustard, mint, and some seasoning.
   Press a third of the crust on top of the
   meat on each lamb rack.

4 Roast the lamb for 15–20 minutes for
   pink meat, or longer if you prefer it
   more well done. Transfer the racks
   to a board, cover loosely with foil,
   and leave to rest for 5 minutes before
   carving and serving.

FREEZE AHEAD

To make the lamb ahead and freeze,
prepare the meat to the end of step
3 up to one month in advance. Wrap
the baking sheet in plastic wrap,
then freeze. To serve, thaw the lamb
overnight in the refrigerator, then
unwrap and complete from step 4.

Serves 6

Moroccan Roasted Rack of Lamb

Prep time: 10 minutes
Cooking time: about 25 minutes, plus resting

1 large bunch of cilantro

½ cup pine nuts, fried in 1 tbsp. olive oil

1 garlic clove, crushed

2 racks of lamb, excess fat trimmed off

2 tbsp. harissa

salt and freshly ground black pepper

Saffron Couscous to serve (see below)

1 Put six cilantro sprigs for the garnish to one side and chop the rest roughly. Put the cilantro, pine nuts, and garlic into a mini food processor and blend to a coarse paste, or crush with a mortar and pestle.

2 Season the lamb and smear the curved side of each rack with the harissa. Press the pine nut and cilantro mixture on top of the harissa. Cover and chill until needed.

3 Heat the oven to 400°F (350°F convection oven). Put the lamb into a roasting pan and roast for 20-25 minutes until the meat is just cooked and tender, yet slightly pink. Slice each rack into chops and serve with couscous, garnished with the reserved cilantro.

Saffron Couscous

Put 1 heaped cup couscous and ½ cup raisins into a large bowl. Add a large pinch of saffron, ½ tsp. salt, and plenty of ground black pepper. Pour 1 cup + 2 tbsp. (250ml) hot vegetable stock over the top, stir, cover, and leave for 10 minutes so the couscous swells and absorbs the liquid. To serve, stir in 2 tbsp. toasted slivered almonds.

Serves 4

Guard of Honor with Hazelnut and Herb Crust

Prep time: 30 minutes
Cooking time: about 45 minutes, plus resting

2 racks of lamb, excess fat trimmed off

salt and freshly ground black pepper

roasted root vegetables to serve

For the hazelnut and herb crust

1½ cups fresh bread crumbs made from Italian bread, such as ciabatta

2 tbsp. each freshly chopped flat-leaf parsley and thyme

1 tbsp. freshly chopped rosemary

2 garlic cloves, crushed

2 tbsp. olive oil

⅓ cup toasted and roughly chopped hazelnuts

4 tbsp. Dijon mustard

1 Heat the oven to 400°F (350°F convection oven). Trim off as much of the fat from the lamb as possible and put the fat to one side. Season the lamb well with ground black pepper.

2 Melt the reserved fat in a large heavy-bottomed skillet, add the lamb, and sear on both sides. Remove the lamb from the pan and leave until cool enough to handle. Put the racks together so the ribs interlock. Place the lamb in a roasting pan, rib bones uppermost, with the lamb fat. Roast for 10 minutes.

3 Meanwhile, make the hazelnut crust. Combine the bread crumbs, herbs, garlic, oil, and seasoning for 30 seconds in a food processor, then add the hazelnuts and pulse for 30 seconds longer.

4 Remove the lamb from the oven and spread the fatty side with the mustard. Press the hazelnut crust onto the mustard.

5 Baste the lamb with the fat in the roasting pan and put back in the oven for 15–20 minutes for rare, 20–25 minutes for medium-rare, and 25–30 minutes for well done. When cooked, remove from the oven, cover loosely with foil, and leave in a warm place for 10 minutes to rest. Carve and arrange the lamb on a serving platter and serve with a selection of roasted root vegetables.

SAVE TIME

Prepare the lamb to the end of step 4. Cool quickly and chill for up to 24 hours. To use, return the lamb to room temperature, then heat the oven and continue with step 5.

Serves 4

Herbed Lamb Chops

Prep time: 10 minutes
Cooking time: about 14 minutes

12 lamb loin chops

1½ tbsp. Dijon mustard

a large handful of fresh parsley, chopped

a large handful of fresh mint, chopped

salt and freshly ground black pepper

boiled new potatoes and a salad to serve

1 Brush the lamb chops with mustard and sprinkle a little seasoning over them.

2 Mix the parsley with the mint in a small bowl, then tip on to a plate. Dip each side of the lamb chops in the herbs, then put onto a nonstick baking sheet. Turn on the broiler.

3 Broil the chops for 10–14 minutes, depending on the thickness and how you prefer your meat cooked, turning once. Serve with boiled new potatoes and salad.

SAVE EFFORT

Use any combination of freshly chopped herbs you like – cilantro, chives and rosemary all work well.

Serves 4

Perfect Beef

Classic Roast Beef with Yorkshire Pudding

Prep time: 20 minutes
Cooking time: about 2 hours, plus resting

4lb. (1.8kg) boned and rolled top round
    roast at room temperature

1 tbsp. all-purpose flour

1 tbsp. mustard powder

salt and freshly ground black pepper

fresh thyme sprigs to garnish

Yorkshire Pudding (see opposite) and
    vegetables to serve

For the gravy

5 tbsp. dry red wine

2½ cups (600ml) beef stock

1   Heat the oven to 450°F (425°F convection oven). Put the beef into a roasting pan, with the thickest part of the fat on top. Mix the flour with the mustard powder, salt, and ground black pepper. Rub the mixture over the beef.

2   Roast the beef in the middle of the oven for 30 minutes.

3   Baste the beef and reduce the oven temperature to 375°F (325°F convection oven). Roast for about 1 hour longer, basting occasionally. Meanwhile, prepare the Yorkshire pudding batter (see opposite).

4   Transfer the beef to a warm carving dish, cover loosely with foil, and leave to rest in a warm place. Increase the oven temperature to 425°F (400°F convection oven) and cook the Yorkshire Pudding.

5   Meanwhile, make the gravy. Skim off any remaining fat from the roasting pan. Put the pan on the stovetop over high heat, add the wine, and boil until syrupy. Pour in the stock, bring to a boil and, again, boil until syrupy: there should be about 2 cups + 2 tbsp. (500ml) gravy. Taste and adjust the seasoning.

6 Carve the beef into slices. Garnish with thyme and serve with the gravy, Yorkshire Pudding, and vegetables of your choice.

Yorkshire Pudding

Sift 1 cup all-purpose flour and ½ tsp. salt into a bowl. Mix in ⅔ cup (160ml) milk, then add 2 beaten large eggs, and season with ground black pepper. Beat until smooth, then whisk in another ⅔ cup (160ml) milk. Remove about 3 tbsp. fat from the beef roasting pan and use to grease 8–12 individual Yorkshire Pudding pans or the holes of a muffin pan. Put the pans into a heated oven at 425°F (400°F convectoin oven) for 5 minutes, or until the fat is almost smoking. Pour the batter into the holes in the pans. Bake for 15–20 minutes until well risen, golden and crisp. Serve immediately.

Serves 8

Roast Rolled Sirloin of Beef with Port Gravy

Prep time: 20 minutes, plus marinating
Cooking time: about 50 minutes – 1½ hours (depending on thickness of meat), plus resting

3¼–4½lb. (1.5–2kg) rolled boneless top sirloin butt roast (chateaubriand)

4 fresh rosemary sprigs, leaves removed and finely chopped

2 garlic cloves, finely chopped

2 tbsp. olive oil

salt and freshly ground black pepper

For the gravy

2 tbsp. all-purpose flour

1¾ cups (400ml) beef stock

7 tbsp. port wine

1 tbsp. red currant jelly

1   Weigh the beef and calculate the roasting time, allowing 5–15 minutes per 1lb. (450g) depending on how well you like it cooked (rare to well done). Put the beef into a roasting pan just large enough to hold the roast. Mix the rosemary with the garlic, oil, and lots of seasoning. Rub the mixture over the roast, then cover with plastic wrap or foil and leave to marinate for 1–3 hours.

2   When the beef has marinated, heat the oven to 400°F (350°F convection oven). Roast the beef for 20 minutes, then reduce the oven temperature to 350°F (325°F convection oven) and roast for the remaining calculated time.

3   When the beef is cooked to your liking, transfer it to a board, cover loosely with foil, and leave to rest for 30 minutes.

4   To make the gravy, tilt the roasting pan and spoon out most of the fat. Put the pan on the stovetop over medium heat and stir in the flour. Cook for 1 minute, mixing well, then gradually stir in the stock. Bubble for 3 minutes, stirring occasionally, then pour in the port. Scrape the bottom of the pan to release the sticky bits and simmer for 5 minutes. Add the red currant jelly

and stir until it dissolves, then strain through a fine mesh strainer into a clean pan. Check the seasoning.

5 Reheat the gravy and serve with the roast beef.

SAVE TIME

Prepare the beef to the end of step 1 up to a day ahead. Cover and chill. Take the beef out of the refrigerator 40 minutes before roasting to let it return to room temperature, then complete the recipe.

Serves 6–8

Perfect Cold Roast Beef

TAKE 5

Prep time: 15 minutes, plus overnight chilling
Cooking time: about 2 hours

4½lb. (2kg) rolled boneless top round roast at room temperature

2 tbsp. light brown soft sugar

1 tbsp. mustard powder

1 tbsp. vegetable oil

coleslaw, watercress leaves, and creamed horseradish to serve

1 Heat the oven to 400°F (350°F convection oven). Pat the beef dry with paper towels and take a note of its weight (just in case). Mix the sugar and mustard powder in a small bowl and rub all over the beef. Heat the oil in a large skillet over high heat and fry the beef until brown on all sides.

2 Sit the beef in a roasting pan just large enough to hold the roast and cover loosely with foil. Roast in the oven for 15 minutes per 1¼lb. (550g) for rare meat, 20 minutes per 1¼lb. (500g) for medium-rare meat, or 25 minutes per 1¼lb. (550g) for well-done meat, then roast for an extra 10 minutes on top of the calculated time. Or use a meat thermometer—for medium-rare meat the internal temperature of the beef should be 140°F.

3 Transfer the beef to a board and leave to cool completely. Wrap well in foil and chill in the refrigerator overnight. (You can also serve this beef hot as part of a buffet meal—just leave it to rest for 30 minutes after roasting, then carve.)

4 An hour before serving, slice the beef thinly and arrange on a platter, then cover. Serve with coleslaw, watercress leaves, and creamed horseradish.

SAVE TIME

Cook the beef to the end of step 3 up to three days ahead, then chill until you are ready to slice.

Serves 8

Boneless Rib Roast with Mustard, Parsley, and Onion Crust

Prep time: 20 minutes
Cooking time: about 2 hours, plus resting

1 large onion, finely chopped

²/₃ cup (160ml) red wine or dry sherry

5lb. (2.3kg) rolled boneless rib roast
at room temperature

2 tbsp. mustard

2 tbsp. freshly chopped flat-leaf parsley

salt and freshly ground black pepper

roasted root vegetables and green
vegetables to serve

SAVE TIME

Prepare the onion mixture to the
end of step 1, then cool, cover, and
chill for up to 24 hours. Complete
steps 2, 3, and 4 to finish the recipe.

1 Heat the oven to 475°F (425°F
convection oven). Put the onion into a
skillet with the wine or sherry. Bring
to a boil and bubble slowly until most
of the liquid evaporates. Remove the
skillet from the heat, then leave the
onion to cool.

2 Put the beef into a large roasting
pan and season all over with black
pepper. Roast (without any extra
fat) for 30 minutes. Reduce the
oven temperature to 375°F (325°F
convection oven) and roast for
15 minutes per 1lb. (450g) longer
for rare, plus 15 minutes extra for
medium-rare or 30 minutes extra for
well-done meat.

3 About 10 minutes before the beef
is cooked, transfer the roast to a
smaller pan, keeping the large pan
containing all the juices for the gravy
(see page 158). Smear the mustard all
over the beef. Add the parsley to the

cooled onion mixture, season with salt and ground black pepper, and press on to the beef. Put back in the oven to finish cooking.

4   Transfer the cooked beef to a warm carving dish, cover loosely with foil, and leave to rest for 30 minutes before serving. Carve the meat into slices and serve with roasted root vegetables and green vegetables.

Serves 6

Perfect Preparation

Follow these tried-and-true directions for trimming, tying,
and larding roasts. You won't go wrong.

Trimming

1 Cut off the excess fat to leave
   a layer about ¼in. (0.5cm)
   thick. (This isn't necessary for
   particularly lean cuts.)
2 Trim away any pieces of meat
   or sinew left by the butcher.
3 If the roast has a covering of fat,
   you can lightly score it—taking
   care not to cut into the meat—
   to help the fat drain away
   during roasting.

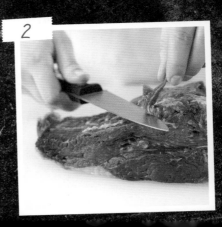

Tying

Tie the roast if you are using a boned and rolled joint, or if you have boned the meat but want to roast it using the bones as a "roasting rack."

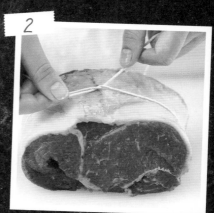

1 Tie a piece of string around the length of the roast, securing it to the bones if they haven't been cut away. If you are preparing a boned and rolled joint, turn it 90 degrees, then tie another piece of string the same way.
2 Starting at one end of the roast, loop string around the meat and tie it securely and firmly. Cut it off and make another loop about 2in. (5cm) from the first.
3 Continue tying the roast this way along the whole length of the meat until it is neatly and firmly secured.

Larding

Threading narrow strips of fat through lean joints of beef helps to guarantee juiciness. The fat is threaded through the roast using a larding needle, which is available from specialist kitchen stores.

1 Cut long strips of pork fat, preferably back fat, which will fit easily into the larding needle.
2 Push the needle right through the roast, so that the tip sticks out at least 2in. (5cm) through the other side.
3 Take a strip of fat, place it in the hollow of the larding needle and feed it into the tip. When the fat can't go in any farther, press down on the meat and pull the needle out. The fat should stay inside.
4 Repeat at 1in. (2.5cm) intervals all around the roast.

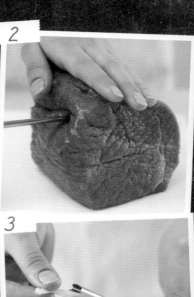

Larding tips

- ☐ Larding is much easier if the strips of fat are very cold or even frozen.
- ☐ The strips of fat don't need to be as long as the roast: you can put several pieces of fat in a single larding channel.
- ☐ Use one strip per 1in. (2.5cm), measuring the longer side of the roast.

Beef roasting times

Heat the oven to 425°F (400°F convection oven). Weigh the roast to calculate the roasting time. Brown the beef in the hot oven for 20 minutes, then turn the oven down to 375°F (325°F convection oven) and roast for the calculated time.

	COOKING TIME PER 1LB. (450G)
Rare	15 minutes
Medium	20 minutes
Well done	25 minutes

Use the times given as a guideline, but remember that cooking times will vary depending on how the meat has been aged and stored, the shape and thickness of the roast, and personal taste. Ovens vary as well. If a recipe gives a different oven temperature, follow the recipe for timing.

How to tell if beef is cooked

To check if roast beef is cooked as you like it, insert a thin skewer into the middle and press out some juices. The juices that run out indicate the stage to which the beef is cooked: red juices for rare, pink for medium-rare, or clear for well done.

Resting

When the beef is cooked, cover loosely with foil and leave to rest for 30 minutes before carving. Larger roasts can rest for up to 45 minutes without getting cold.

Beef Tenderloin with Mushrooms and Chestnuts

Prep time: 20 minutes, plus 2–3 hours marinating
Cooking time: 45 minutes, plus resting

2¼lb. (1kg) beef tenderloin, trimmed

7 tbsp. butter

1½ cups (350ml) beef or veal stock

2 tbsp. mixed peppercorns, crushed

1 shallot, finely chopped

1 tbsp. vegetable oil

1lb. (450g) mixed wild mushrooms, cleaned and trimmed

heaped 1 cup cooked and peeled (or vacuum-packed) chestnuts, halved

3 tbsp. freshly chopped flat-leaf parsley

salt and freshly ground black pepper

For the marinade

1¾ cups (400ml) red wine

4 tbsp. Madeira

2 tbsp. balsamic vinegar

5 large shallots, sliced

1 bay leaf

1 fresh thyme sprig

1 Put the beef in a bowl, add the marinade ingredients, cover, and leave in a cool place for 2–3 hours. Remove the shallots and beef with a slotted spoon; keep the liquid. Pat the beef dry with paper towels. Melt 2 tbsp. butter in a pan and slowly fry the shallots. Add the marinade and boil until reduced to one-third. Add the stock and boil to reduce to one-third. Discard the bay and thyme. Set the sauce aside.

2 Heat the oven to 400°F (350°F convection oven). Roll the beef in the crushed peppercorns. Heat the oil in a heavy-bottomed skillet and brown the beef over high heat. Put the beef in a roasting pan and roast for 25 minutes for medium-rare. Put the meat on a board, cover with foil, and leave to rest for 10 minutes.

3   Melt 2 tbsp. butter in a pan and
    cook the shallot until soft. Add the
    mushrooms and sauté until the liquid
    evaporates. Stir in the chestnuts and
    parsley, then season and set aside.
    Reheat the sauce and whisk in the
    remaining butter. Carve the beef and
    serve with the mushrooms, chestnuts,
    and sauce.

Serves 6

Beef Tenderloin in Pastry

Prep time: 1 hour, plus soaking and chilling
Cooking time: about 1¼ hours, plus cooling and resting

2¼–3lb. (1–1.4kg) beef tenderloin, trimmed

4 tbsp. butter

2 shallots, chopped

½oz. (15g) dried porcini mushrooms, soaked in 7 tbsp. boiling water

2 garlic cloves, chopped

3 cups finely chopped flat mushrooms

2 tsp. freshly chopped thyme, plus extra sprigs to garnish

6oz. (175g) chicken liver pâté

6oz. (175g) thinly sliced prosciutto

13oz. (375g) store bought puff pastry dough, fresh or thawed

all-purpose flour to dust

1 large egg, beaten

salt and freshly ground black pepper

Red Wine Sauce to serve (see page 118)

1   Season the beef with salt and ground black pepper. Melt 2 tbsp. of the butter in a large skillet and, when foaming, add the beef and cook for 4–5 minutes to brown all over. Transfer to a plate and leave to cool.

2   Melt the remaining butter in the wiped-out pan, add the shallots, and cook for 1 minute. Drain the porcini mushrooms, putting the liquid to one side, and chop them. Add them to the pan with the garlic, the reserved liquid, and the fresh mushrooms. Turn up the heat and cook until the liquid evaporates, then season with salt and pepper and add the chopped thyme. Leave to cool.

3 Put the chicken liver pâté into a bowl and beat until smooth. Add the mushroom mixture and stir well. Spread half the mushroom mixture evenly over one side of the beef. Lay half the prosciutto on a piece of plastic wrap, overlapping the slices. Invert the mushroom-topped beef onto the ham. Spread the remaining mushroom mixture on the other side of the beef, then lay the rest of the prosciutto, also overlapping, on top of the mushroom mixture. Wrap the beef in the plastic wrap to form a firm, thick sausage shape and chill for 30 minutes. Heat the oven to 425°F (400°F convection oven).

4 Cut off one-third of the pastry dough and roll out on a lightly floured work surface to ⅛in. (0.3cm) thick and 1in. (2.5cm) larger than the beef. Prick all over with a fork. Transfer to a cookie sheet and bake for 12–15 minutes until brown and crisp. Leave to cool, then trim to the size of the beef and place on the cookie sheet. Remove the plastic from the beef, brush with the beaten egg and place on the baked pastry.

5   Roll out the remaining dough into a 10 × 12in. (25.5 × 30.5cm) rectangle. Roll a lattice dough cutter over the dough and gently ease the lattice open. Cover the beef with the lattice, tuck the ends under, and seal the edges. Brush with the beaten egg, then roast for 40 minutes for rare to medium, or 45 minutes for medium. Leave to rest for 10 minutes before carving. Garnish with thyme sprigs and serve with Red Wine Sauce.

Red Wine Sauce

Soften 2 cups finely chopped shallots in 2 tbsp. olive oil for 5 minutes. Add 3 chopped garlic cloves and 3 tbsp. tomato paste and cook for 1 minute. Add 2 tbsp. balsamic vinegar and simmer briskly until very little liquid is left, then add ¾ cup + 2 tbsp. (200ml) dry red wine and continue simmering to reduce by half. Pour in 2½ cups (600ml) beef stock and bring to a boil, then reduce the heat and simmer until the sauce reduces by one-third. Season to taste wth salt and ground black pepper, then reheat, if necessary, and serve.

Stuffed Top Round of Beef

Prep time: 35 minutes, plus marinating
Cooking time: about 1½ hours, plus resting

3lb. (1.4kg) top round roast

1 tbsp. balsamic vinegar

2 tbsp. white wine vinegar

3 tbsp. olive oil

3 tbsp. freshly chopped marjoram
  or thyme

2 red bell peppers, seeded and quartered

1 heaped cup fresh spinach, cooked and
  well drained

½ cup pitted black olives, chopped

⅓ cup chopped smoked ham

½ cup raisins or golden raisins

salt and freshly ground black pepper

roast potatoes and vegetables to serve

1 Make a deep cut along the beef to
   create a pocket, then put it into a dish.
   Combine the vinegars, oil, marjoram
   or thyme, and some ground black
   pepper. Pour over the beef and into
   the pocket. Marinate in a cool place
   for 4–6 hours, or overnight.

2 Turn on the broiler. Broil the peppers,
   skin-side up, under the broiler until
   the skins char. Put into a bowl, cover,

and leave to cool, then remove the
skins.

3 Squeeze the excess water from the
   spinach, then chop and put it into
   a bowl with the olives, ham, and
   raisins. Mix well and season with salt
   and ground black pepper.

4 Heat the oven to 375°C (325°F
   convection oven). Line the pocket of
   the beef with the peppers, reserving
   two pepper quarters for the gravy.
   Spoon the spinach mixture into the
   pocket and spread evenly. Reshape
   the meat and securely tie at regular
   intervals with string (see page 111).

5 Put the beef into a roasting pan just
   large enough to hold the roast. Pour
   the marinade over and roast for
   1 hour for rare, or 1¼ hours for
   medium-rare, basting from time
   to time. Transfer the beef to a board,
   cover loosely with foil, and leave
   to rest while you make the gravy.

6 Skim off the excess fat from the
   roasting pan. Put the pan on the

stovetop over high heat and bring the pan juices to a boil. Add ½ cup (125ml) water and boil for 2–3 minutes. Finely chop the reserved pepper pieces and add to the gravy.

7 Carve the beef and serve with the gravy, roast potatoes, and vegetables of your choice.

Serves 6

Spiced Beef

Prep time: 20 minutes, plus soaking
Cooking time: about 5 hours, plus cooling

4lb. (1.8kg) boneless, salted bottom
round roast or silverside roast

1 onion, sliced

4 carrots, sliced

1 small turnip, sliced

1–2 celery stalks, chopped

8 cloves

packed ½ cup light brown sugar

½ tsp. mustard powder

1 tsp. ground cinnamon

juice of 1 orange

1   Soak the meat for several hours, or overnight, in enough cold water to cover it to remove the saltiness.

2   Drain and rinse the meat, then put it into a large, heavy-bottomed pan with the vegetables. Add water to cover the meat and bring slowly to a boil. Skim off any scum, then cover with a lid, reduce the heat, and simmer for 4 hours. Leave the meat to cool completely in the liquid.

3   Heat the oven to 350°F (325°F convection oven). Drain the meat well, then put into a roasting pan and press the cloves into the fat. Mix the sugar with the mustard, cinnamon, and orange juice, then spread it over the meat.

4   Roast for 45 minutes–1 hour, basting from time to time. Serve hot or cold.

Serves 6

Vegetable Dishes

White Nut Roast

Prep time: 20 minutes,
Cooking time: about 1 hour plus cooling

3 tbsp. butter, plus a little extra
  to grease

1 onion, finely chopped

1 garlic clove, crushed

2½ cups mixed white nuts, such as
  brazil nuts, macadamias, pine nuts,
  and whole almonds, ground in a food
  processor

2 cups fresh white bread crumbs

grated zest and juice of ½ lemon

¾ cup grated Parmesan

⅔ cup roughly cooked and peeled
  (or vacuum-packed) chestnuts,
  roughly chopped

1 cup drained artichoke hearts in oil,
  roughly chopped

1 large egg, lightly beaten

2 tsp. each freshly chopped parsley, sage,
  and thyme, plus extra sprigs

salt and freshly ground black pepper

1. Heat the oven to 400°F (350°F convection oven). Melt the butter in a pan and cook the onion and garlic for 5 minutes, or until soft. Put into a large bowl and leave to cool.

2. Add the nuts, bread crumbs, lemon zest and juice, cheese, chestnuts, and artichokes to the cool onion mixture. Season well and bind together with the beaten egg. Gently stir in the chopped herbs.

3. Put the mixture onto a large piece of buttered aluminum foil and shape into a fat sausage, packing tightly. Scatter with the extra herb sprigs and wrap in the foil.

4. Place on a cookie sheet and roast for 35 minutes, then unwrap the foil slightly and continue cooking for 15 minutes longer, or until turning golden. Serve cut into thick slices.

FREEZE AHEAD

To make ahead and freeze, prepare the nut roast to the end of step 3, then cool, cover, and freeze for up to one month. Cook from frozen for 45 minutes, then unwrap the foil slightly and roast for 15 minutes longer until turning golden.

Serves 8

Red Cabbage Timbales with Mushroom Stuffing

Prep time: 1 hour
Cooking time: 1 hour, plus cooling

3lb (1.4kg) red cabbage
Mushroom and Cashew Stuffing (see
  opposite)
3 tbsp. butter
2½ cups finely chopped onions
3 tbsp. balsamic vinegar
salt and freshly ground black pepper
small fresh thyme sprigs to garnish
  (optional)
green vegetables to serve

For the sauce
4 tbsp. sugar
4 tbsp. red wine vinegar
⅔ cup (160ml) dry red wine
1 tbsp. lemon juice

1   Put the cabbage into a large pan of
    boiling water. Bring back to a boil,
    then reduce the heat and simmer
    until the outside leaves are soft
    enough to be eased away. Lift the
    cabbage out of the pan; keep the
    water. Remove three outer leaves
    and boil them for 3–4 minutes longer,
    then place in a bowl of cold water.
    Quarter the whole cabbage and
    remove the core. Take 1½lb. (700g) of
    the cabbage and remove and discard
    any thick central vein, then shred the
    leaves very finely, cover, and put to
    one side.

2   Heat the oven to 375°F (325°F
    convection oven). Line six ⅔-cup
    (160ml) molds with plastic wrap. Drain
    the whole cabbage leaves and cut in
    half; discard the central veins. Use the
    leaves to line the molds. Fill each mold
    with stuffing and then cover with foil.
    Place in a large roasting pan and pour
    in enough warm water to come halfway
    up the sides of the molds. Carefully
    transfer the pan to the oven and cook
    for 30 minutes, or until just set in the
    middle.

3   Meanwhile, melt the butter in a

128

pan, add the onions, and cook until soft. Mix in the shredded cabbage, vinegar, and 3 tbsp. water. Season well. Cook, stirring from time to time, for 15–20 minutes until just tender.

4 To make the sauce, put the sugar and vinegar into a pan. Cook over low heat until the sugar dissolves, then bring to a boil and cook to a rich caramel. Pour in the wine and leave to reduce by half, then add lemon juice to taste and season. Cool.

5 Turn out the timbales, spoon shredded cabbage on top and around, drizzle with sauce, and garnish with thyme, if you like. Serve with green vegetables.

Mushroom and Cashew Nut Stuffing

Melt 4 tbsp. butter in a pan, add 1⅓ cups finely chopped onions and cook until soft and golden. Add 3 cups roughly chopped cremini mushrooms and fry over medium heat until the moisture evaporates. Stir in ¾ cup roughly chopped salted cashews, 4 tbsp. freshly chopped flat-leaf parsley, and 2 cups fresh bread crumbs. Leave to cool, then stir in 2 extra-large beaten eggs and season with salt and freshly ground black pepper. Mix well, then cover and put to one side. This stuffing can also be used for chicken or turkey.

Serves 6

Roasted Stuffed Peppers

Prep time: 20 minutes
Cooking time: about 50 minutes

4 tbsp. butter

4 sweet peppers with stems on, halved
and seeded

3 tbsp. olive oil

4 cups roughly chopped cremini
mushrooms

4 tbsp. finely snipped fresh chives

3½oz. (100g) feta

1 cup fresh white bread crumbs

2 tbsp. freshly grated Parmesan

salt and freshly ground black pepper

1 Heat the oven to 350°F (325°F convection oven). Use a little of the butter to grease a baking sheet or shallow baking dish and put the peppers in it side by side, ready to be filled.

2 Melt the remaining butter with 1 tbsp. of the oil in a pan. Add the mushrooms and fry until golden and there isn't any excess liquid left in the pan. Stir in the chives, then spoon the mixture into the pepper halves.

3 Crumble the feta over the mushrooms. Mix the bread crumbs and Parmesan in a bowl, then sprinkle over the peppers. Season with salt and ground black pepper and drizzle with the remaining oil.

4 Roast in the oven for 45 minutes, or until golden and tender. Serve warm.

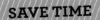

SAVE TIME

Complete the recipe up to one day ahead, then cover and chill. To serve, reheat under the broiler for 5 minutes.

Serves 8

Stuffed Pumpkin

Prep time: about 40 minutes
Cooking time: about 1 hour 50 minutes, plus standing

3–4lb. (1.4–1.8kg) pumpkin

2 tbsp. olive oil

2 leeks, trimmed and chopped

2 garlic cloves, crushed

2 tbsp. freshly chopped thyme leaves

2 tsp. paprika

1 tsp. ground turmeric

heaped ½ cup long-grain rice,
    cooked and drained

2 tomatoes, peeled, seeded and diced

4 tbsp. toasted and roughly chopped
    cashews

1 cup grated cheddar

salt and freshly ground black pepper

1   Cut a 2in. (5cm) slice from the top of
    the pumpkin and put to one side for
    the lid. Scoop out and discard the
    seeds. Using a knife and a spoon,
    cut out most of the pumpkin flesh,
    leaving a thin shell. Cut the flesh into
    small pieces and put to one side.

2   Heat the oil in a large pan, add the
    leeks, garlic, thyme, paprika, and
    turmeric and fry for 10 minutes. Add
    the chopped pumpkin flesh and
    fry for 10 minutes longer, or until
    golden, stirring frequently to prevent
    sticking. Transfer the mixture
    to a bowl. Heat the oven to 350°F
    (325°F convection oven).

3   Add the pumpkin mixture to the
    cooked rice along with the tomatoes,
    cashews, and cheese. Fork through
    to mix and season with salt and
    ground black pepper.

4   Spoon the stuffing mixture into
    the pumpkin shell, top with the lid,
    and bake for 1¼–1½ hours until the
    pumpkin is soft and the skin
    is brown. Remove from the oven and
    leave to stand for 10 minutes. Cut into
    wedges to serve.

Sweet Roasted Fennel

Prep time: 10 minutes
Cooking time: about 1 hour

1½lb. (700g) fennel (about 3 bulbs)

3 tbsp. olive oil

4 tbsp. butter, melted

1 lemon, halved

1 tsp. sugar

2 large fresh thyme sprigs

salt and freshly ground black pepper

1   Heat the oven to 400°F (350°F convection oven). Trim and quarter the fennel and put into a large roasting pan.

2   Drizzle the fennel with the oil and melted butter and a squeeze of lemon juice. Add the lemon halves to the roasting pan. Sprinkle with sugar and season generously with salt and ground black pepper. Add the thyme and cover with a damp piece of nonstick parchment paper.

3   Roast for 30 minutes, then remove the parchment paper and roast for 20–30 minutes longer until lightly charred and tender.

Serves 4

Roasted Butternut Squash

Prep time: 15 minutes
Cooking time: 40 minutes

2 butternut squash
2 tbsp. olive oil
2 tbsp. butter
2 tbsp. freshly chopped thyme leaves
1 red chili, seeded and finely chopped
   (see Safety Tip, page 79)
salt and freshly ground black pepper

1 Heat the oven to 425°F (400°F
   convection oven). Cut the squash in
   half lengthwise and scoop out the
   seeds. Cut in half again, then put into
   a roasting pan. Drizzle with the oil,
   season with salt and ground black
   pepper, and roast for 40 minutes.
2 Meanwhile, put the butter into a bowl
   with the thyme and chili and mix
   well. Add a little to each slice
   of the cooked butternut squash.

SAVE EFFORT

For an easy alternative flavor, use
crushed garlic instead of chili.

Sage-Roasted Parsnips, Apples, and Prunes

Prep time: 20 minutes
Cooking time: about 55 minutes

6–8 tbsp. olive oil

4lb. (1.8kg) parsnips, peeled, quartered, and cored

6 apples, peeled, quartered, and cored

16 ready-to-eat pitted prunes

4 tbsp. butter

1–2 tbsp. freshly chopped sage leaves

1–2 tbsp. honey (optional)

salt and freshly ground black pepper

---

1   Heat 3–4 tbsp. of the oil in a large roasting pan, add the parsnips in batches, and fry over medium heat until a rich golden brown all over. Remove from the pan and put to one side. Add 3–4 tbsp. of the oil to the same pan and fry the apples until golden brown. Remove from the pan and put to one side.

2   Heat the oven to 400°F (350°F convection oven). Put the parsnips back into the pan and season with salt and ground black pepper. Put the pan in the oven and roast for 15 minutes.

3   Add the apples and continue roasting for 10 minutes. Add the prunes to the pan and roast for 5 minutes longer. At the end of this time, test the apples. If they are still firm, roast everything for 5–10 minutes longer until the apples are soft and fluffy.

4   Put the pan on the stovetop over very low heat. Add the butter and sage, drizzle with honey, if you like, and spoon into a hot serving dish.

SAVE TIME

Prepare the parsnips and apples to the end of step 1, then cool, cover, and chill for up to one day. Complete steps 2, 3, and 4 to finish the recipe and serve hot.

Sides, Sauces, and Gravies

Roasted Mediterranean Vegetables

Prep time: 10 minutes
Cooking time: about 40 minutes

4 plum tomatoes, halved

2 onions, quartered

4 red bell peppers, seeded and cut into strips

2 zucchini, thickly sliced

4 garlic cloves, unpeeled

6 tbsp. olive oil

1 tbsp. freshly chopped thyme leaves

sea salt flakes and freshly ground black pepper

1 Heat the oven to 425°F (400°F convection oven). Put the tomatoes into a large roasting pan with the onions, peppers, zucchini, and garlic. Drizzle with the oil and sprinkle with thyme, sea salt, and ground black pepper.

2 Roast, turning occasionally, for 35–40 minutes until tender. Serve hot or at room temperature.

HEALTHY TIP

To make a nutritionally complete meal, sprinkle with toasted sesame seeds and serve with hummus.

Mustard-roasted Potatoes and Parsnips

TAKE 5

🍴 **Prep time:** 25 minutes
Cooking time: about 1¼ hours

3lb. (1.4kg) small, even-size potatoes, scrubbed

1¾lb. (800g) small parsnips, peeled

4 tbsp. goose fat

1–2 tbsp. black mustard seeds

1 tbsp. sea salt

1 Cut out small wedges from one side of each of the potatoes and parsnips (this will help make them extra crisp). Put them into a pan of salted, cold water, bring to a boil, and boil for 6 minutes. Drain well.

2 Heat the oven to 400°F (350°F convection oven). Heat the goose fat in a roasting pan for 4–5 minutes until sizzling hot. Add the potatoes and toss in the fat, then roast for 30 minutes. Add the parsnips and sprinkle with the mustard seeds and sea salt. Roast for 30–35 minutes longer, turning all the vegetables after 20 minutes, until they are golden outside and tender throughout.

FREEZE AHEAD

Prepare the vegetables to the end of step 1. Spread them out on a baking sheet and leave to cool, then freeze on the sheet. Once frozen, put them into a freezer bag and freeze for up to three months. To use, cook from frozen, allowing an additional 15–20 minutes total cooking time.

Serves 8

Roasted Baby Potatoes

Prep time: 3 minutes
Cooking time: about 35 minutes

2¼ lb. (1kg) baby potatoes

2 tbsp. olive oil

salt and freshly ground black pepper

1 Heat the oven to 425°F (400°F convection oven). Tip the potatoes into a roasting pan and drizzle with oil. Season well with salt and pepper and toss gently to mix.

2 Roast the potatoes for 30–35 minutes, tossing occasionally, until tender. Serve immediately.

SAVE EFFORT

Prepare the potatoes to the end of step 1 up to 3 hours ahead. Cover and store at cool room temperature. Complete step 2 to roast, then serve.

Serves 6

Spiced Red Cabbage

Prep time: 10 minutes
Cooking time: about 15 minutes

1 tbsp. olive oil

1 tbsp. butter

½–1 tsp. each ground ginger and
coriander, to taste

1lb. (450g) red cabbage, cored and finely
shredded

2 tbsp. balsamic vinegar

1 tbsp. sugar

a large handful of fresh parsley, roughly
chopped

salt and freshly ground black pepper

1 Heat the oil and butter in a large pan
over high heat. Stir in the spices and
cook for 1 minute. Add the cabbage
and cook for 10 minutes, stirring often,
or until just soft.

2 Pour in the vinegar and sugar and
cook for 3 minutes. Stir in the parsley
and check the seasoning. Serve
immediately.

SAVE TIME

Complete steps 1 and 2, without
adding the parsley, up to 3 hours
ahead. Cover and chill. To serve,
reheat gently in a pan, then add the
parsley and seasoning.

Serves 6

Roasted Root Vegetables

Prep time: 15 minutes
Cooking time: about 1 hour

1 large potato, cut into large chunks

1 large sweet potato, cut into
   large chunks

3 carrots, cut into large chunks

4 small parsnips, halved lengthwise

1 small rutabaga, cut into large chunks

3 tbsp. olive oil

2 fresh rosemary sprigs

2 fresh thyme sprigs

salt and freshly ground black pepper

1 Heat the oven to 400°F (350°F convection oven). Put all the vegetables into a large roasting pan. Add the oil.

2 Use scissors to snip the herbs over the vegetables, then season with salt and ground black pepper and toss everything together. Roast for 1 hour, or until tender. Serve immediately.

SAVE EFFORT

An easy way to get a brand new dish is to use other combinations of vegetables: try celeriac instead of parsnips, fennel instead of rutabaga, and peeled shallots instead of carrots.

Tomatoes with Thyme

Prep time: 3 minutes
Cooking time: about 12 minutes

1¼lb. (550g) cherry tomatoes on the vine

1 tbsp. olive oil

3 fresh thyme sprigs

salt and freshly ground black pepper

1 Heat the oven to 425°F (400°F convection oven). Trim the tomatoes into small bunches and put the bunches into a small roasting pan. Drizzle with the oil, add the thyme, and season well with salt and ground black pepper.

2 Roast for 10–12 minutes until the tomatoes have burst but are still holding their shape. Remove the thyme and serve immediately.

SAVE TIME

Prepare the tomatoes to the end of step 1 up to 3 hours ahead. Cover and store at cool room temperature, then complete step 2 to serve.

Serves 6

Perfect Stock

Good stock can make the difference between a good dish and a great one. Homemade stock adds depth of flavor to many dishes.

Vegetable Stock

For 4½ cups (1.1 liters), you will need: 1½ cups each chopped onions, celery, leeks, and carrots; 2 bay leaves; a few fresh thyme sprigs; 1 small bunch of fresh parsley; 10 black peppercorns; ½ tsp. salt.

1 Put all the ingredients into a large pan and add 7 cups (1.7 liters) cold water. Bring slowly to a boil and skim the surface.

2 Partially cover the pan, then reduce the heat and simmer for 30 minutes. Adjust the seasoning, if necessary. Strain the stock through a fine strainer into a bowl and leave to cool. Cover and chill in the refrigerator for up to three days. Use as required.

Basic Bone Stock

For 3¾–4½ cups (900ml–1.1 liters), you will need:
2lb. (900g) meat bones, fresh or from cooked meat; 2 chopped onions; 2 chopped carrots; 1 tsp. salt; 3 black peppercorns; and 1 bouquet garni (1 bay leaf and a few fresh parsley and thyme sprigs).

1   Chop the bones. Put them in a pan with 2 quarts (2 liters) water, the vegetables, salt, peppercorns, and herbs. Bring to a boil and skim off any scum. Cover and simmer for about 3 hours. Strain the stock and, when cold, remove all traces of fat.

Chicken Stock

For 4½ cups (1.1 liters), you will need:
3½lb. (1.6kg) chicken bones; 8oz. (225g) sliced onions; 8oz. (225g) sliced celery; 1 cup chopped leeks; 1 bouquet garni (2 bay leaves, a few fresh thyme sprigs, and a small bunch of fresh parsley); 1 tsp. black peppercorns; ½ tsp. salt.

1   Put all the ingredients into a large pan and add 3 quarts (3 liters) cold water. Bring slowly to a boil, then skim the surface.
2   Partially cover the pan, then reduce the heat and simmer slowly for 2 hours. Adjust the seasoning, if necessary.
3   Strain through a cheesecloth-lined srainer into a bowl and cool quickly. Cover and chill in the refrigerator for up to three days. Use as required. Degrease (see page 156) before using.

Giblet Stock

To make 1½ quarts (1.5 liters), you will need:

turkey giblets; 1 quartered onion; 1 halved carrot; 1 halved celery rib; 6 black peppercorns; 1 bay leaf.

1 Put all the ingredients into a pan and add 6½ cups (1.5 liters) cold water. Cover and bring to a boil.

2 Reduce the heat and simmer for 30 minutes–1 hour, skimming occasionally. Strain through a fine strainer into a bowl and cool quickly. Cover and chill for up to two days.

Degreasing stock

Meat and poultry stock needs to be degreased—vegetable stock does not. You can remove the fat from the surface using paper towels, but the following methods are easier and more effective. There are three main methods for degreasing: ladling, pouring, and chilling.

1 **Ladling** While the stock is warm, place a ladle on the surface. Press down and allow the fat floating on the surface to trickle over the edge until the ladle is full. Discard the fat, then repeat until all the fat has been removed.

1

2 **Pouring** For this you need a degreasing pitcher or a double-pouring gravy boat, which has the spout at the bottom of the vessel. When you fill the pitcher or gravy boat with a fatty liquid, the fat rises. When you pour, the stock comes out while the fat stays behind in the pitcher.

3 **Chilling** This technique works best with stock made from meat, because the fat solidifies when cold. Put the stock in the refrigerator until the fat becomes solid, then use a slotted spoon to remove the pieces of fat.

3

Classic Gravy

Prep time: 2 minutes
Cooking time: 10 minutes

juices in the roasting pan

about 2 tbsp. all-purpose flour

about 4½ cups (1.1 liters) stock (see
pages 154–6)

salt and freshly ground black pepper

1 Make the gravy while the meat
or poultry is resting. Tilt the roasting
pan to tip the liquid into one corner.
Spoon off most of the fat, leaving
about 2 tbsp. fat and the juices
in the pan.

2 Put the roasting pan on the stovetop
over low heat and add the flour. Stir it
in with a wooden spoon or whisk and
cook for 1–2 minutes. Don't worry if it
looks lumpy at this point.

3 Gradually pour in the stock, stirring
it in with a whisk. Bring the gravy
to a boil, whisking all the time, then
let it simmer and reduce a little to
concentrate the flavor. Taste, season,
and keep warm until ready to serve.

Serves 8

Basic Gravy

To make about 1¼ cups (300ml), you will need:
juices in the roasting pan; 1¼–2 cups (300–450ml) vegetable water, or chicken, vegetable, or meat stock (see pages 154–6); salt and freshly ground black pepper.

1 While the meat or poultry is resting, tilt the roasting pan and carefully pour (or skim) off the fat from one corner, leaving just the dark brown juices. Put the pan on the stovetop over medium heat and pour in the vegetable water or stock as appropriate.

2 Stir thoroughly, scraping up the sediment, then bring to a boil and boil steadily, stirring all the time, until the gravy is a rich brown color. Taste, season, and keep warm until ready to serve.

Thick Gravy Sprinkle 1–2 tbsp. all-pupose flour into the roasting pan and cook, stirring, until brown, then gradually stir in the liquid and cook, stirring, for 2–3 minutes until smooth and slightly thicker.

Rich Madeira Gravy

To serve eight, you will need:
juices in the roasting pan; ⅓ cup
all-purpose flour; ⅔ cup (160ml)
Madeira; about 4½ cups (1.1 liters)
stock (see pages 154–6); 2 tbsp. red
currant jelly; salt and freshly ground
black pepper.

1   While the meat or poultry is
    resting, tilt the roasting pan and
    pour off as much of the fat as you
    can, leaving just the dark brown
    juices. Put the pan on the stovetop
    over low heat, add the flour and
    stir for 2 minutes, then stir in the
    Madeira and bubble for 1 minute.
2   Gradually pour in the stock
    and mix in, scraping up all the
    goodness from the bottom of the
    pan. Bring to a boil, then add the
    red currant jelly, reduce the heat,
    and simmer for 5 minutes. Taste
    and season, then pour through
    a strainer into a gravy boat and
    keep warm until ready to serve.

Rich Red Wine Gravy

This rich gravy goes well with
roasted chicken or meat, such as beef.

To serve eight, you will need:
4 tbsp. all-purpose flour; 1¼ cups
(300ml) red wine; 4½ cups (1.1 liters)
chicken or beef stock; and salt and
freshly ground black pepper.

1   While the meat or poultry is
    resting, strain the juices from the
    roasting pan into a bowl and skim
    off any fat, keeping 3 tbsp. of the
    fat to one side.
2   Put the fat back into the pan
    and whisk in the flour. Cook
    over medium heat until the flour
    browns. Take the pan off the heat
    and stir in the wine until smooth,
    then bubble for 2–3 minutes.
3   Stir in the chicken or meat juices
    and the stock. Bring to a boil, then
    bubble for 10–15 minutes until
    the gravy reduces by half and
    is smooth. Skim off any fat and
    season with salt and ground black
    pepper. Keep warm until ready
    to serve.

White Wine Gravy

Perfect served with roast chicken.
To serve eight, you will need:
4 tbsp. all-purpose flour; 2 cups +
2 tbsp. (500ml) chicken stock (see
page 155); 2 tbsp. red currant jelly; salt
and freshly ground black pepper.

1   While the chicken is resting, tilt
    the roasting pan and carefully
    pour (or skim) off the fat from one
    corner, leaving just the dark brown
    juices. Spoon 3 tbsp. of the juices
    into a bowl and mix with the flour
    to make a paste.

2   Pour the chicken stock, white
    wine, and red currant jelly into
    the roasting pan and scrape the
    residue from the bottom of the pan
    using a wooden spoon.

3   Put the pan on the stovetop over
    low heat and whisk in the flour
    mixture. Simmer slowly for
    5–10 minutes, then season
    to taste with salt and black pepper
    and keep warm until ready
    to serve.

Mustard and Honey Gravy

If you don't like turkey giblet stock, use good chicken stock instead. Honey helps to disguise the bitterness from overbrowned turkey juices.

To serve eight, you will need:
3½ tbsp. all-purpose flour; 1½ tbsp. honey; 6 tbsp. white wine; 3¼ cups (750ml) hot turkey stock (see right); ½–1 tbsp. wholegrain mustard.

SAVE TIME

Make the gravy up to 1 hour ahead. Strain into a small pan; set aside. Slowly reheat when needed.

1   Pour off all but 2 tbsp. of the fat from the turkey roasting pan, leaving behind all the dark juices. Put the pan on the stovetop over medium heat and stir in the flour and honey. Cook, stirring constantly, for 1 minute.

2   Gradually mix in the wine, then the stock. Cook, stirring constantly, until thicker. Simmer for a few minutes. Add any juices from the resting meat. Strain, then stir in the mustard to taste. Serve in a warm gravy boat.

Turkey Stock for Mustard and Honey Gravy

Put the turkey giblets into a large pan. Add 1 sliced onion; 2 chopped carrots; 1 chopped celery rib; 10 peppercorns; 2 bay leaves; 3 fresh thyme sprigs; and 6¾ cups (1.6 liters) cold water. Bring to a boil, then simmer for 1 hour. Pour through a fine mesh strainer lined with paper towels. Cool, then pour into an airtight container and chill for up to 1 day. This recipe makes about 3 cups + 2 tbsp. (700ml).

Applesauce

The perfect accompaniment for roasted pork or goose.

To serve eight, you will need:
2lb. (900g) cooking apples, such as McIntosh, peeled, cored, and roughly chopped; 4 tbsp. butter, 4 tbsp. light brown sugar, or to taste.

1 Put the apples into a pan with 4–6 tbsp. water. Cover and cook over low heat for about 10 minutes, stirring occasionally, until the apples are soft and reduced to a pulp.
2 Beat with a wooden spoon until smooth, then rub through a medium or fine strainer, if you like. Stir in the butter and 2 tbsp. of the sugar, then taste and add a little more sugar, if you like. Serve warm, at room temperature, or chilled.

FREEZE AHEAD

To make ahead and freeze, complete the recipe, then cool and put into a freezer container. Label and freeze for up to one month. To use, thaw at cool room temperature. Put into a pan and simmer over medium heat for 2–3 minutes until heated through.